THE METAL GUIDE TO THE BIBLE

BIBLE READING NOTES

JONATHAN BRANT

TO INSPIRE
COURAGE SPIRIT CHARACTER

yfc   CWR

METTLE GUIDE TO THE BIBLE

m
mettle

BIBLE READING NOTES

TO INSPIRE
COURAGE SPIRIT CHARACTER

yfc | CWR

CONTENTS

SUPERBUR

BIBLIOTECA UNIVERSALE RIZZOLI

RICHARD BACH
BIPLANO
L'autore di
IL GABBIANO
JONATHAN LIVINGSTON

SUPERBUR

BIBLIOTECA UNIVERSALE RIZZOLI

RICHARD BACH
STRANIERO
ALLA
TERRA

L'autore di
IL GABBIANO
JONATHAN LIVINGSTON

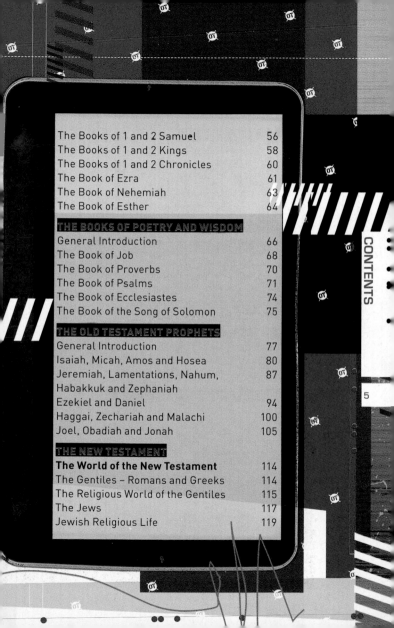

CONTENTS

6

Do you have digital or cable TV? At first it's so exciting: 'Oh boy! There's twenty-four hours a day of Hungarian soaps on channel 307, and a nail-bitingly exciting armadillo tossing contest on the sports channel!'

Soon, though, you come to realise that the *really* good programmes are on special channels, and you have to pay extra if you want to watch them.

I once lived with a family that had cable TV, and sometimes, when I became bored of the armadillo throwing, I would try to watch the special channels. In those days, even if you hadn't paid the 'extra' it was just about possible to tell what was going on.

'Yep, that's definitely basketball. Oh, no wait, I think it's that new Eddie Murphy film ...' Occasionally there was even a moment of total and beautiful clarity: 'That's not Eddie Murphy, it's the Queen of England!'

8

But generally you were peering through a thick fog, the characters' feet were at the top of the screen, their heads were at the bottom, and there were thick wavy lines running all through the middle. A less than satisfying viewing experience!

Sometimes, reading the Bible is a lot like trying to watch cable TV without a decoder. The story, or the teaching, seems to appear and disappear through a thick fog. We think we know what's going on, but to be honest we're not quite sure. The characters seem boring and dull, and what on earth does all of this have to do with us anyway?

Still we just plough on, waiting for that one moment of beautiful clarity when God speaks to us through a particular word or verse – then we plunge back into the fog. It is our hope that to some extent this book will function like a decoder for you when you come to read the Bible.

BUT WHY SHOULD I NEED A DECODER?

You might be thinking, 'But if the Bible is God's Word, surely the Holy Spirit will decode it for me – I don't need books.' Well, that's true. The Holy Spirit does give us moments of total, beautiful clarity, but God also expects us to make some effort ourselves. That's part of His plan for us.

Here's something to think about. If you travelled back in time, just the twenty years to when I was in school, you would find that much of the playground conversation is completely unintelligible.

Think of slang – would you be insulted or pleased to be called a 'Tavare', or an 'Oscar'?

What about TV programmes – could you discuss the plot of *Dallas*, or laugh at jokes about the Fonz in *Happy Days*? Was 'Adam Ant' a kiddies creation like Scooby Doo, or a famous singer?

People's lifestyles and interests change very quickly, even in the space of twenty years, so it's interesting to remember that the most recent parts of the Bible were written 2,000 years ago. Don't worry, though. God has made sure that even though it was written in different languages to ours, by people who would never have dreamt of cars, or factories, let alone computers, mobile phones or space travel, we can all understand something of what is being said. With a little bit of effort we can understand so much more.

It is particularly useful to know how the people of the Bible lived, what they liked and disliked, what they were afraid of and what their concerns were.

And if we know something of when and why a particular book of the Bible was written, what we read will make much more sense.

Now, does that make sense?

HOW TO USE THIS BOOK

A friend of mine was a complete boffin when it came to maths and sciences, but thick as two short planks in English. He had to sit his English exam three times before he passed!

One of the reasons he kept failing was that he insisted his best chance of getting through was to memorise whole chunks from the *Letts Revise English* book. When he walked into an exam his brain was bursting with the memorised beginning and ending of a story (he was just going to fill in the middle), and paragraphs of criticism on all of the syllabus' books. It never occurred to him that the examiners might have seen *Letts Revise* once or twice before, or that he would be making better use of his time if he actually sat down and read one of the set books.

You might laugh, but that is a common approach to Bible study. We like the Bible study notes, but we never actually get around to reading the Bible. OK, this is probably better than nothing, but even better would be actually getting stuck into the Bible.

Some things were just made to go together: Big Macs and French fries; Tom and Jerry; this book and the Bible! Ideally you should read with this book in one hand and the Bible in the other. The whole purpose is to help you understand the Bible better and learn more about what God is saying through it as you read.

It's a two-way street. You might start by reading the Bible, and then turn to this book to find more background information on what you're reading about. Or you could drive in the other direction by starting with this book, then looking up the parts that it recommends you read in the Bible.

GENERAL

Each book of the Old Testament is covered in *this* book, so whatever you are reading you should be able to look it up in the Contents and turn straight to the right page to find the information you want.

Most of the books are covered in the order they appear in your Bible, but not all. So don't panic if you can't find one in its usual place - it's in there somewhere.

GENERAL INTRODUCTIONS

The books are dealt with in groups that make them easier to understand - eg, all the prophetic books together, and all the historical books together. At the beginning of each section is a general introduction. It might be worth having a look at these to get an idea of the kind of books you are reading.

Once you reach the sections on individual books you will find a number of different paragraphs. Here is what you will find under each heading:

INTRODUCTION

Like the blurb on the back of a book or a DVD, this is intended to give you an idea of what the book is about and hopefully catch your interest so that you will want to read on.

GROUND COVERED

Maps come in different scales – some cover a few miles in intense detail, others cover the whole world generally. The paragraphs under this heading are like a global map – the entire book fitted onto a postcard! In a few words it tells you what is going on in the book as a whole.

MAIN THEME

If you read the Bible quite often you'll know that sometimes it's almost impossible to see the wood for the trees. You think, 'But what on earth does this mean?

Why is this story here at all?' Some of the books are so long, and cover so many different stories and topics, that it is impossible to guess at what the overall message is.

This paragraph attempts to sum up for you what we might learn from the book as a whole if we had the time and energy to read it from cover to cover in one go.

You can then keep this in mind as you read bits of it and hopefully see where individual stories fit into the overall message.

BUT WHAT ABOUT ME?

At school it's easier to enjoy a subject when you can see how it will help you in life. If you want to become a rocket scientist and work for NASA then physics becomes exciting. If, however, your dream is to be a fashion designer, then the 'conductability coefficient of plastic' doesn't hold many thrills.

This paragraph tries to show how each one of the books of the Bible has important lessons for us today. After you've read 'But what about me?' you should be better able to apply the contents of the book to your own life and situation. This will hopefully make what you're reading more exciting.

INTERESTING BITS/CHARACTERS

This is possibly the most important and helpful information of all, because it will help you to pick up the Bible and explore new territory. These lists should lead you through the minefield of difficult or confusing parts into the heart of the Bible book you're reading. If there's a person that you're especially interested in, or a story that you particularly want to read, you should find it here.

Many of the passages listed here are the bits that are underlined in my own Bible – the parts I have found interesting in the past. They are just a taster, and won't include everything in the book that is important and exciting. As you read more you could add your own 'Interesting bits' to the list.

LITTLE AND OFTEN

Some restaurants advertise that if you can eat your way through the entire menu then you eat for free. For snakes (which can eat one huge meal and then digest it for weeks afterwards) that would be a cheap way to live – slither in once a month, and then slide (rather more slowly) home to digest all that free food. But that's not how we humans work – we must eat little and often.

It's the same with Bible reading. What we need is to dip into the Bible as often as possible, but not wear ourselves out by doing too much at once. Don't worry if you don't stick to your plans, just keep going or try something new. Whatever you do, just don't stop!

READ PAST, PRESENT AND FUTURE

I want to suggest to you a time traveller's way of reading the Bible which will hopefully make it easier to understand and apply to your life. When you read a few verses in the Bible and want to know what they mean to you, try this approach.

Past – Ask yourself questions about when the verses were originally written. What was going on in Israel's history for instance? Then ask yourself: 'What might the author have been trying to communicate about God to the people who first read this book?' The section on 'Main theme' could help you here.

Present – Next, ask yourself what the verses could mean to you today. The 'But what about me?' section might be able to help you with this part.

Future – Finally, ask yourself: 'What am I going to do, or think, differently in the future in the light of what these verses of the Bible say to me?'

If we read the Bible like this we will be allowing God to speak to us and, more importantly, acting on what He says to us!

14

WHAT'S SO SPECIAL ABOUT THE BIBLE?

DANGER: CREATIVE GENIUS AT WORK!

Can you imagine living in a monochrome world? A universe with only one colour?

Fortunately, the God who created the universe we live in is a creative genius. Our world is not black and white but an incredible multicolour paradise. The latest printers and monitors claim to be able to reproduce millions of colours, but those are just a fraction of the colours that God has placed in the world around us.

God went wild! Like some sort of mad professor, He was never content with just doing the job – it had to be fantastic, beautiful, outrageous and extreme.

Just think of all the different tastes, different animals, different landscapes, different smells – and compare Arnold Schwarzenegger with Angelina Jolie. The world is full of the weird and the wonderful!

NOW LET ME INTRODUCE MYSELF ...

Now just imagine that that incredible, creative genius wanted to tell you about Himself, and give you some clues about the world He had made and that you were living in. Imagine that He decided to communicate to you through a book. Would He write a boring book? No way! The Bible – God's number one way of revealing Himself to us – is like the world we live in: a work of genius.

WHAT WILL I FIND IN THE BIBLE?

The Bible is chock full of the mysterious and the bizarre: talking donkeys; fingers appearing and writing cryptic messages at kings' banquets; and the awesome teacher and prophet who could turn water into wine and feed thousands of people by multiplying food.

But it's not all the stuff of tabloid news headlines. There are epic tales of war and bloodthirsty battle. For the romantics, heroes are everywhere: brave boys defeat terrible giants; wise leaders save their countries from destruction; beautiful women risk everything to change the course of history; and true friends chance their lives to help each other.

BUT THERE IS A PROBLEM

As you read this you might be thinking, 'Well, if the Bible is so popular and so exciting, why do I find it so hard to read and understand?'

The truth is, the Bible is far more exciting and interesting than a simple textbook, but it needs more effort to understand. Like most things in life, the more you put in, the more you will get out. As any football lover knows, to play well, or be part of a good team, requires planned and disciplined effort – just kicking a ball around occasionally won't cut it. We need to know something about the background of the various parts of the Bible before we can fully understand it and enjoy it.

Here is some very basic information about the Bible as a whole ...

THAT BIG BLACK BOOK ON YOUR SHELF

If you were to pull down a Bible off your shelf and open it up you would find that it is not just one continuous stream of words – it is divided up. Good thing too, because all together it is one long, long book. There are over 750,000 words, which is equal to about twenty of the novels you might normally choose to read.

The first and biggest division is between the two 'Testaments'. As you probably know, these are called the 'Old Testament' and the 'New Testament'.

The word 'testament' really means agreement or relationship.

The Old Testament is about the agreement that God made with the ancient nation of Israel.

The New Testament is about the fresh agreement that God made with all people through Jesus Christ.

Each Testament is then broken down into separate books – thirty-nine in the Old and twenty-seven in the New.

There are two more divisions which make it much easier to find particular sections. They are the divisions of the books into chapters and verses. These weren't put there by the authors, but were added very much later when the Bible began to be printed in large numbers.

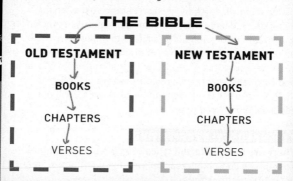

THE BIBLE

OLD TESTAMENT

BOOKS

CHAPTERS

VERSES

NEW TESTAMENT

BOOKS

CHAPTERS

VERSES

BUT WHO WROTE ALL THOSE BOOKS?

If God ran a Job Centre He might make some pretty strange appointments as He obviously has His own ideas about what qualifies people to do a certain job. For example, if we wanted people to write a book for us we would probably choose those with degrees in English and experience as journalists.

But the people that God 'employed' to write His book were from all different walks of life. Some, like Moses and Paul, were highly educated scholars. Some were professionally religious – priests and prophets like Jeremiah and Ezekiel. Still others were normal working men, fishermen like Peter, doctors like Luke, or farmers like Amos. There were even kings, like David and Solomon, who had a hand in writing certain books.

SO IT'S NOT REALLY GOD'S BOOK AT ALL THEN?

There are some things in this life that will always remain mysteries.

Why are dinosaurs extinct? Why do we suffer some kind

of instantaneous brain retardation when we try to speak to a fit member of the opposite sex? And how, exactly, did God inspire the writers of the Bible? We will probably never fully understand.

One verse, 2 Timothy 3:16, proves God's involvement in its writing, saying that 'all Scripture is God-breathed' – but that doesn't help much on the 'how' front.

One thing we do know: it wasn't some sort of divine dictation. God used the particular personality, experiences and situations of each of the writers to make their book unique. But God guided each of them in such a way that each one revealed an important part about God's character and His plans, and the way that He works in the world.

This means that it is absolutely correct to think of the Bible as God's Word to us.

TYPES AND STYLES OF WRITING

There are many different types of writing in the Bible. To impress an English teacher you might call them 'genres' of writing. For example:

History – where the deeds of kings and the political experiences of the nations of Israel are recorded.

Prophecy – where God tells people what He thinks about events in the present, and what will happen in the future.

Proverbs – where wise advice is stated in short, sometimes funny, sayings so that it will not be forgotten.

Poetry – almost everyone can quote at least a line or two from the poem/psalm that begins 'The Lord is my shepherd'.

Biography – where the words and actions of Jesus are recorded by people who had known Him and heard His teaching.

Songs – songs of love in the Song of Solomon, which contains the unbeatable line 'Your teeth are white like newly sheared sheep just coming in from their bath'; and songs of praise to God, some of which we still sing today.

BUT IS IT TRUE?

Imagine a tough London policeman interviewing witnesses to a bank robbery. If every witness walked into the office, sat down and described what had happened in exactly the same words as the others, the policeman would begin to suspect a conspiracy. It simply doesn't work that way. Honest witnesses will argue over the colour of the getaway car, the height of the robber, and particularly the order in which things happened. They are human after all, not video cameras. The police expect such differences. No criminal would ever have been convicted if witnesses were considered unreliable because of different recollections of this sort.

It's precisely the same with the Bible. The very few and small disagreements over minor facts, that opponents of the Bible are always quoting, just make it certain that the Bible isn't a hoax – it hasn't been carefully altered to make it look more reliable.

THE BIG ISSUES

Consider these issues: the origin of the universe; whether God exists; is humanity basically good or evil? what happens when you die?

If you were to discuss those issues in class, or even just with a few friends, there would be a huge argument. Billy thinks we're all descended from spacemen. Mary is convinced that humans are basically good because her baby niece is just so sweet. Alfred the scientist reckons we're just animals.

Yet all the authors of the Bible are in perfect agreement about these issues and many more equally complex ones. Add to this the fact that no archaeological dig has ever discovered anything that would disprove the history of the Bible, and you should have more than enough evidence to conclude that the Bible is true.

BUT THERE IS MORE – CHANGED LIVES

The best evidence that can be given for the Bible being truly God's book is the fact that it has such a powerful effect on people's lives. Many, many people have been converted to Christianity simply by reading the Bible. It has a habit of suddenly coming alive in the minds of people reading it and totally changing all their previous thoughts and understanding about life.

It is because of this that there are millions of people around the world today who consider the Bible their most treasured possession. Risks are taken each day to smuggle Bibles into countries such as Iran and North Korea that are closed to Christianity. The reason is that Christians within those countries are literally desperate for God's Word. No other book has quite that effect on people.

No other book is God's Word.

MAPS OF THE OLD TESTAMENT REGION

CASPIAN SEA
NINEVAH
EUPHRATES RIVER
TIGRIS RIVER
MEDITERRANEAN SEA
SAMARIA
BABEL (OR BABYLON)
SUSA
JERUSALEM
EGYPT
PERSIAN GULF
NILE RIVER

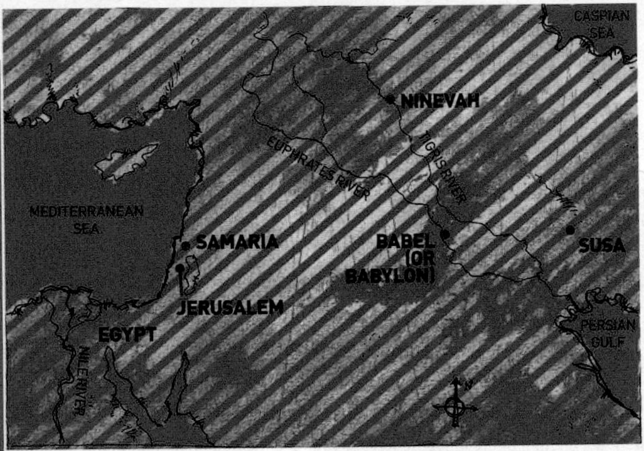

ANCIENT MAP OF THE NEAR EAST

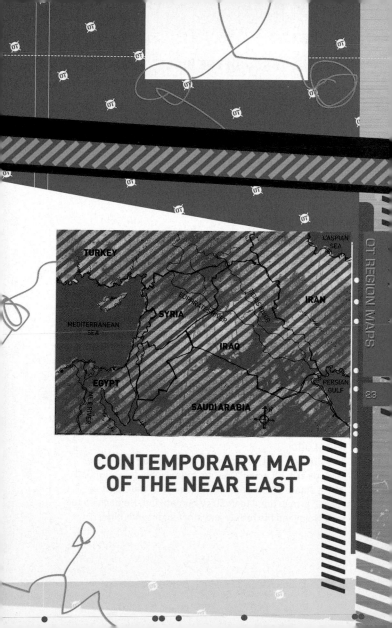

**CONTEMPORARY MAP
OF THE NEAR EAST**

A SCROLL THROUGH THE BIBLE

PART 1: IN THE BEGINNING ...

THE STORY SO FAR ...

There *is* no story so far!

'Hey, man, that's just, like, well cosmic. Yaahh, cosmic!'
You might rather be dead, or seen wearing false chest
hair, than be heard using such an outdated hippie word as
cosmic, but there is no other word to describe the events of
the first twelve chapters of Genesis.

CREATION

Genesis starts in an awesome way when God, simply by
speaking the words, creates the entire cosmos – our time,
our space, our universe, our solar system, our planet, and
everything in it – including humans.

THE FALL

When Adam and Eve disobey God by munching on the one
thing God didn't put on the menu, the consequences are
cosmic. From now on there will be a barrier between man
and God, and the natural way of things will be for all men
and women everywhere to disobey and displease, rather
than obey and please God. Fortunately, God promised right
there in the garden that one day He would make things right
again. We call this THE PLAN.

THE FLOOD

This little episode could well have been the end of the
human race if it wasn't for one man, Noah, to whom God
took a shine. When God sent a flood of ... wait for it ...
cosmic proportions to destroy humankind, He decided to
save Noah and his family and start again with him.

ABRAHAM

When the US Marines go recruiting, they look for people made of 'the right stuff'. God was looking for a man with just what it takes to be His follower. Abraham proved he had 'the right stuff' when he heard God's voice, and trusted Him enough to do what He said.

A GREAT NATION

Later God said to Abraham, 'I have a plan – I call it THE PLAN – that is going to be good news for all the people of the world. Your children are going to become a great nation, and through them I'm going to carry out THE PLAN.'

'Wow,' said Abraham. 'That sounds a bit of all right, but me and the missus don't have no kids and we're well past our sell-by dates, if you know what I mean!'

They soon learnt that when it comes to THE PLAN, nothing is too hard for God. It wasn't long before little Isaac was 'cooing and pooing' like any other little baby.

A GRANDSON AND GREATGRANDSONS

Isaac grew up, passed his exams, got a job and settled down with a nice girl called Rebekah. They had twin sons called Esau and Jacob. Jacob was the one God had chosen to be the father of His special people.

One day God bumped into Jacob in the desert and changed his name to Israel. His descendants then became known as the children of Israel, or the Israelites.

PART 2: THE ISRAELITES IN EGYPT

THE STORY SO FAR ...

The world is in a mess, but God has THE PLAN to make it right. He's chosen the man who is going to be the father of God's special accomplices in THE PLAN. His name is Israel, his children are the children of Israel, and his wife is Mrs Israel.

JOSEPH

One of Jacob/Israel's sons was called Joseph (who has since become famous through that popular Andrew Lloyd Webber musical). He was a very talented young man, but so bigheaded that he had to turn sideways to fit through doors. Joseph was a favourite of his dad, but not at all popular with his many brothers. Eventually, they got completely fed up with Joseph and decided to get rid of him. Killing him would have given them the most pleasure, but selling him into slavery meant more money and less blood – such brotherly kindness.

JOSEPH IN EGYPT

In Egypt, Joseph's life was a rollercoaster of pleasant and unpleasant experiences.

God was with him, though, and in the end not only was he cured of his chronic big head, but he ended up as Pharaoh's right-hand man.

THE FAMILY COME TO STAY

Do you remember THE PLAN? This is where it becomes obvious that God had been at work behind the scenes keeping His plan on track.

There was an incredible drought. We're not just talking hosepipe bans here – we're talking less moisture than a cream cracker in a tumble dryer. Soon the drought turned into a famine. The only country in the world with anything like enough food was Egypt. People came from all over to beg, including Joseph's brothers. While other people were turned away and whole nations died out, the children of Israel were saved because Joseph forgave his brothers the little slavery fiasco and invited everyone to come and live with him.

OI! WE'RE NOT SLAVES, WE'RE GUESTS
The Bible says that a Pharaoh came to power who didn't remember Joseph.

He put the Israelites to work making bricks and building ... pyramids, of course! The Egyptians worked the Israelites hard and treated them cruelly, but no matter what happened the Israelites kept multiplying like rabbits. In the end the Egyptians decided that every Israelite boy that was born must be thrown into the river.

MOSES
Sometimes you can bend the rules a little. One Israelite family threw their baby boy into the river all right, but they gave him his own little boat. This little sea-dog was called Moses, the person that God was going to use to help His people escape from Egypt. He was found 'messing about on the river' by one of Pharaoh's daughters, who raised him in the palace of Pharaoh.

Moses wondered what he could do to help his people. The answer was: not a lot. When he killed an Egyptian, he fled the country wearing dark glasses and a wig as he slipped through customs.

GOD TAKES OVER
Fortunately, Moses didn't have to do it on his own. God wanted His people out of Egypt, and He was happy to help things along a little.

When Moses returned, God started sending plagues on Egypt. It was soon decided that it would be better for everyone concerned if the Israelites just left.

So they packed their bags and their animals and marched out of Egypt. They had come in as one small, starving family - they marched out as a whole nation.

PART 3: THE PROMISED LAND

THE STORY SO FAR ...

The world is in a mess, but God has THE PLAN to make it right. The children of Israel are His chosen accomplices, and now they are out of Egypt and have become a mighty nation. But where will they live?

INTRODUCTIONS

God and the Israelites arranged a little rendezvous at a spot in the desert called Mount Sinai. Moses spoke for the Israelites, and God spoke for Himself. A few ground rules were set down, and then it was full speed ahead for the land that God had promised Abraham that his children's children would live in.

A LITTLE BIT LOST

Sadly, things didn't quite go according to plan. It looked so simple on paper, but when it came to push and shove the Israelites found themselves lacking faith in God and confidence in themselves. They were too scared of the big, ugly people already living in the land to go in and fight for it.

So instead they wandered for forty years in a small and barren wilderness, carrying God's tent around with them.

THAT'S NOT THE END OF THE STORY, THOUGH

God was not amused with their cowardice and grumbling, but He kept them alive by feeding them manna from heaven and making drinking fountains flow out of rocks when they were thirsty. He hadn't come this far in THE PLAN only to give up because of a yellow streak in some of the people He had chosen.

A NEW GENERATION

God doesn't age at all, so He's quite willing to wait. Since one generation of Israelites were jelly-kneed cowards, He simply allowed the next generation to grow up. Forty years later this generation had had enough of living in tents in the wilderness, and they trusted God enough to be willing to fight for the promised land.

JOSHUA

They were led by an amazing man called Joshua. Joshua had been Moses' assistant for many years, and was well suited to the job in hand. He was part James Bond (all-action hero and military commander), part Nelson Mandela (intelligent and charismatic politician), and part Billy Graham (man of God).

After Moses' death, Joshua led the people across the River Jordan into the promised land.

THIS TOWN AIN'T BIG ENOUGH FOR THE TWO OF US, PARDNER!

God had told His people that it wasn't just a matter of moving in alongside the people already living in the promised land – they were to wipe them out completely.

This meant plenty of opportunities for Joshua to exercise his James Bond qualities as he led the children of Israel into battle after battle. When walls of great cities fell down at a shout (like Jericho) and the sun stood still in the sky, it became obvious that God was rather stacking the deck in the Israelites' favour.

OH, THAT'S GOOD ENOUGH, ISN'T IT?

The Israelites soon got bored of all that fighting. What they really wanted was to settle down in little bungalows with a nice view and enjoy the land full of milk and honey that they had fought for.

Joshua put his Nelson Mandela hat on and carefully divided up the land so that each of the twelve tribes had its own patch to live in.

PART 4: JUDGES AND KINGS

THE STORY SO FAR ...

The world is in a mess, but God has THE PLAN to make
things right again. The Israelites, the people God has
chosen to be His accomplices in THE PLAN, are finally
living in the promised land. But their laziness is going to
cause them some problems ...

WHAT'S 'IS NAME AGAIN?

The Israelites were a forgetful bunch, and after only a few
years of living in luxury in the promised land they forgot all
about God and all about THE PLAN, which was the reason
they were there in the first place.

IF THAT'S THE WAY YOU WANT IT ...

God decided to let the Israelites see how they liked life
without Him.

He allowed the people the Israelites had been too lazy
to drive out of the land to attack and rob and steal from
them. This got the Israelites' attention, because suddenly
life wasn't so luxurious any more. Someone else was eating
their milk and honey.

The Israelites had a remarkable recovery of memory.
Now they remembered God who had given them the land
in the first place, and they called out to Him to help them
again: 'Help! They've stolen our milk and honey!'

THE JUDGES

When the people cried out to Him, God would raise up a
Judge – a man or a woman with similar qualities to Joshua.
This Judge would defeat the enemies, restore political
order, and lead the people back to God. This occurred
again, and again, and again, for about 400 years!

DOWN WITH THE JUDGES, UP WITH THE KINGS

Finally the Israelites had had it – right up to here – with the
whole Judges saga, and so for that matter had God. God

told Samuel, the last of the Judges, to anoint a young man named Saul to be the first king of Israel.

SAUL

'Isn't he a good looking chap? So tall and strong – I bet he could give those filthy Philistines a good thrashing. He's just the sort of man we want for king!'

Saul looked the part, but he wasn't quite the man that God wanted.

DAVID

When Saul had offended God one time too many, Samuel anointed a new king called David. Saul didn't particularly like the idea of David becoming king, as he was rather partial to the job himself. So Saul chased David all over the country. He should have known that it is never a good idea to get in God's way when He's working on THE PLAN.

A CLUE, A CLUE!

The next piece of THE PLAN came to light when Saul had died and David had become king.

God told David that from his descendants would come One whom God would call His Son, and who would reign as a king forever and forever. Now, who might that be?

SOLOMON

When David died, his wise son Solomon became king of Israel.

In his time, the nation of Israel became fabulously wealthy and was known through all the earth as a splendid destination for both holidays and study trips.

Things had never looked better as far as THE PLAN was concerned, but they didn't stay that way for long.

When Solomon died, his son, Rehoboam, became king. The new king suffered a bit of a hot flush and became power crazed, coming over all big and macho. He decided that he would beat his people into submission.

WELL, WE'LL PLAY ON OUR OWN THEN!

This bit of carefully considered politics didn't have quite the effect that Rehoboam had hoped. Instead of scaring the people into obeying his every command, it made them angry. The northen tribes decided they would start their own country without him. They stormed off to their own homes in the northern part of the promised land and made a much nicer man, called Jeroboam, their king.

TWO NATIONS, TWO KINGS, TWO ALTARS

From this time on God's special people, the Israelites, were split into two nations with two of everything. One king ruled the northern kingdom, and one ruled in the southern kingdom.

The people of the northern kingdom worshipped God in a city called Bethel, and the people of the southern kingdom continued to worship at the Temple in Jerusalem.

PART 5: DESTRUCTION
THE STORY SO FAR ...

The world is in a mess, but God has THE PLAN to make things right. His chosen accomplices, the Israelites, have now split into two distinct nations – the northern and the southern kingdoms.

HERE WE GO, HERE WE GO, HERE WE GO!

Now that they were on their own, with their own nation and their own king, the people of the northern kingdom set about getting up God's nose as much as possible.

In fairness, this probably wasn't their actual plan, but they couldn't have done a better job if they'd tried.

WATCH IT!

God wasn't slow in telling them that they were bang out of order. He warned them that if they didn't sort themselves out there would be very nasty consequences, and it would probably end in tears before bedtime.

But the people were enjoying themselves too much to worry about moaning old prophets, and they carried on as if they didn't have a care in the world.

SOMEWHERE TO THE NORTH ...
The people failed to notice the growth of a nation called Assyria to the north of them. The Assyrians were strong and powerful people who were beginning to look with greedy eyes towards their wealthy neighbours.

God had promised he would judge the northern kingdom, and the Assyrians were the very people He was going to use.

R.I.P NORTHERN KINGDOM
Little did the people of the northern kingdom realise that their whole nation was about to be squashed like a banana under a steamroller.

Before they really knew what was happening, the king of Assyria had swept down from the north, defeated all their armies, destroyed their towns and carried all of the people away into captivity. The northern kingdom was no more.

DOWN SOUTH
The kings and people of the southern kingdom were better at following God than the people of the northern kingdom.

'Better, but still not good enough,' said the prophets. 'You've got to learn to follow God all the time, and not just when it suits you.' The southern kingdom were cruising for a bruising.

WE ARE THE CHAMPIONS!
After he had destroyed the northern kingdom, the king of Assyria set his sights on the southern kingdom as a little 'two for the price of one' deal.

Things did not look good for the southern kingdom, but the king of Assyria was about to learn, like others before him, that God was in control and only *He* says what should happen and when. In the middle of the night, an angel from God went out into the middle of the Assyrian army and slaughtered thousands of the soldiers.

While he was walking around the next morning, knee deep in dead bodies, the king of Assyria had a blinding flash of inspiration.

'Something fishy's going on here,' he said, and he hightailed it out of Jerusalem.

WE ARE INVINCIBLE

For a while, this little episode had a good effect on the people of the southern kingdom – they remembered who God was. But soon they were convinced they were invincible. God loved them too much to let anything bad happen to them. They could do whatever they wanted without fear. Wrong!

THE BABYLONIANS

Somewhere to the north, the bully-boy Assyrians were being soundly thrashed by the 'mucho macho' Babylonians. Soon the Babylonians were looking with greedy eyes towards the little nation of Israelites to the south.

One hundred years after the northern kingdom bit the dust, the southern kingdom was wiped out by the Babylonians and the people carried away into captivity.

What had happened to THE PLAN, we ask ourselves?

PART 6: THE RETURN FROM CAPTIVITY
THE STORY SO FAR ...

The world is in a mess, but God has THE PLAN to make things right. Unfortunately His accomplices, the Israelites, are all living in captivity in the cruel empires of the north. Is it all over? Is THE PLAN dead in the water?

DON'T PANIC!

As the people of the southern kingdom were being led into captivity by the Babylonians, things looked pretty darn grim.

There was one voice of hope. The prophet Jeremiah prophesied that the captivity would only last seventy years and then the people would be allowed home. It might not have helped the older ones much, but Jeremiah knew that God still had THE PLAN. It wasn't quite a dead duck yet!

ALL CHANGE
Now that the Babylonians had served their purpose in THE PLAN, God was about to judge them for their cruelty. He raised up a new empire ruled by blokes who were more in touch with their feminine side and not as macho or cruel as the Babylonians. But they were still formidable soldiers, and they gave the Babylonians their come-uppance in no uncertain terms.

Once they were in charge, they allowed the captive peoples to return to their own lands to rebuild their cities and nations.

WE SHALL NOT ... WE SHALL NOT BE MOVED!
Once back in the promised land that God had given them, the Israelites were determined never to be moved out of it again, not by anyone. They had been cured of their tendency to forget God and worship other idols by their horrible experiences of destruction and captivity. They were by no means perfect, but they had finally realised that what made them unique and special was their relationship to the one true God. They wanted to play their part in implementing THE PLAN.

IT'S ALL GONE QUIET ...
For 400 years after the people of the southern kingdom returned to their homes, all was quiet as far as THE PLAN was concerned. Then ...

PART 7: JESUS

THE STORY SO FAR ...

The world is in a mess, but God has THE PLAN to make things right. THE PLAN is about to be fulfilled ...

IT'S A BOY!

One winter's night, some shepherds washing their socks ... I mean, watching the box ... I mean, watching their flocks, were treated to an impromptu concert.

'No,' they were told by the lead singer. 'We're not Israel's entry for the Eurovision Song Contest. We're angels! We're celebrating the birth of a very special baby.'

This little boy, born in a farmyard in an obscure village in Israel, was the end result of all of God's planning over the hundreds of years that He had been working with the Israelites as His accomplices.

The boy, although poor, was an Israelite – of the nation that God had miraculously delivered from Egypt and made His own.

He was of the southern kingdom – whose people God had brought back from terrible exile to live once more in the promised land.

He was a descendant of David – the king to whom God had promised a great, great, great grandson who would rule for ever.

This little baby was Jesus, the only Son of God, the Saviour of the world.

GROWING PAINS?

We don't know much about Jesus' childhood. The Bible gives us one or two snapshots of Him as a boy, but otherwise it just assures us that He 'grew in wisdom and stature and in favour with God and all the people' (Luke 2:52). Perhaps the Bible doesn't tell us any more because this part of Jesus' life isn't as important as the next part ...

LET'S GET TO WORK

Jesus spends His adult life doing some very cool stuff. He heals people, performs miracles, casts out demons and teaches about what it means to know God and follow Him. Jesus gathers twelve disciples to follow Him around, do what He does and learn from Him. Unfortunately, the Romans and the Jewish leaders don't like the way Jesus is shaking up their ideas about God and life in general ...

THE END? THE BEGINNING?

The Jewish leaders have had enough. As far as they're concerned, Jesus is a troublemaker, and they need to get rid of Him. So, they get together with the Romans and plot to have Jesus crucified. But, of course, this was God's PLAN all along. By dying and rising again, Jesus starts to clean up the mess that the world is in and make things right again. He will finish the job one day when He returns as Lord of all creation to rule in peace forever.

THE PLAN CONTINUES

After a simply jaw-dropping resurrection, Jesus goes back to heaven and leaves His (rather scared) disciples to carry on His work. Fortunately for them, Jesus leaves the Holy Spirit to help them out. With the Holy Spirit at work, the Church grows and spreads, and thousands and thousands of people hear about Jesus and decide to follow Him. Which just about brings us to today ...

THE **FIVE** BOOKS

GENERAL INTRODUCTION

ARE THEY WORTH READING?

Owning a double-barrelled name was a huge misfortune at my school, and there was only one person in my year who had one. He also had a rather large nose – that's two misfortunes, which is often all it takes for people to form an opinion. Based on those two pieces of evidence, this guy was invariably known as the 'big nosed snob'. How witty!

Years later – the sixth form to be exact – he became my friend. Not because I was feeling sorry for him, but because he turned out to be a really nice guy. He certainly wasn't a snob, and a big nose is really a very minor issue.

First impressions, especially impressions borrowed from other people, are not very accurate. Don't listen to other people's impressions of the first five books of the Bible. Read them yourself – they're well worth it.

BUT AREN'T THEY BORING AND IRRELEVANT?

'Pages and pages of mindnumbingly tedious laws about not eating pork. Chapter after chapter with instructions about how many tassels there should be per foot on the curtains in the tabernacle.

'Jesus did away with all that Old Testament stuff, so I'm certainly not going to waste my valuable time on it, especially when I could be doing something worthwhile – like watching TV.'

These are common views, but wrong. If we make the effort and go about it in the right way, the first five books of the Bible are among the most interesting and exciting to read.

WHY ARE THEY GROUPED TOGETHER?

'The Law and the Profits' – sounds like the title to some boring documentary about corruption in the police force, doesn't it? Actually, it was what the Jewish people called their Bible. Sorry – that's 'prophets', not 'profits'.

The first five books are what Jewish people call the Law. They are also known as the Five Fifths of Moses, which means that they only make complete sense and tell the whole story when taken together. The title gives us a hint as to who the Jews think wrote them – the greatest prophet and leader of the whole Old Testament, the adopted son of Pharaoh of Egypt and God's chosen deliverer for His people. Yes, you've guessed it – Moses.

The five books cover a period of time that is at the very least as long as the rest of the Bible put together – from the creation of the world, to the coming of the children of Israel to the promised land, and Moses' death. (It makes sense that he would have to stop writing then, doesn't it?)

All of Jewish religion and identity is based upon these books, and they couldn't rate them more highly if they tried.

DO THEY HAVE AN OVERALL THEME?

It might not be right at the top of your 'to do' list yet, but finding someone you want to marry and then persuading them that they want to marry you is no easy task. I won't tell you which part I had the most trouble with.

The main theme of the first five books is God's choosing of Israel to be His special people (not unlike a marriage relationship) and the way He wins her.

Once they've got together, after some very exciting adventures they have to decide on the rules for living happily ever after.

BUT WHAT ABOUT ME?

The New Testament makes it clear that we as Christians are now part of God's chosen people, like the Israelites in the Old Testament. As we read the first five books we can learn a lot about how God wants us to live, and be reassured that He loves us and has chosen us to be His own.

By reading these books, we can understand who we are and what our purpose and place in the world is.

THE BOOK OF
GENESIS

A BOOK WITH ANSWERS FOR THOSE WHO WONDER ABOUT LIFE'S BIG QUESTIONS.

INTRODUCTION

There was a time when films about people suffering from amnesia were popular. But imagine how scary it would be: you wake up in a hospital bed (not a pleasant experience anyway) and don't know who you are.

Now, I know that in real life Aunt Daisy, who'd been sitting by your bed for hours eating all the chocolates, would screech with excitement and be very quick to tell you all about yourself and your wonderful family. But what if she didn't?

As a human race we do suffer from a kind of amnesia. You can't even remember your own birth, can you, let alone the birth of humankind. The book of Genesis is given to us by God to perform the 'Aunt Daisy' role, to remind us of who we are, where we come from, what our purpose is, and what is good and bad.

GROUND COVERED

There are chains of thought that will simply eat your mind alive. For example: 'Does he/she like me?' No matter how much time and thought power you put into that question, no matter how many times you go over all the available evidence – 'He burped when he walked past me in the corridor so he must like me'/'She didn't laugh when I burped in the corridor so she must hate me' – you never come up with an actual answer. Your brain just gets caught in a never-ending loop until it jams like an old school computer on a Friday afternoon.

Genesis is all about questions like that, and as old as it is, it offers answers that even today are still as believable as anything else on offer in the market of ideas. It is particularly about beginnings, which is what 'genesis' means: the beginnings of the universe; the beginnings of humankind; the beginnings of God's chosen people; and the beginnings of God's relationship with humans.

MAIN THEMES ||||||||||||||||||||||||||||||||

The book of Genesis can be split into two parts, both dealing with beginnings.

THE FIRST ELEVEN CHAPTERS

These first chapters deal with the beginnings of the whole universe, and of humankind in particular.

In the form of epic stories, Genesis traces the history of humanity and explains such diverse issues as how sin entered the world, why there are different languages and nations, and how God deals with us when we sin.

CHAPTERS 12–50

Now that the minor matter of the beginning of the universe is out of the way – that didn't take long – we can proceed to the matter of the beginnings of God's chosen people and His plans for them.

We start with a man called Abraham (originally Abram) and finish with his great grandson Joseph.

BUT WHAT ABOUT ME?

Genesis hits on many of the big philosophical questions that non-Christians are asking:

Q. Where do we come from?
Q. Why are we here?
Q. Why is there so much evil and suffering in the world?

MAIN CHARACTERS

Adam and Eve – Read Genesis 1–4
Noah and his ark – Read Genesis 5:28–9:29
Abraham – Read Genesis 12:1–25:11
Joseph – Read Genesis 37:1–50:26

INTERESTING BITS

Creation – Read Genesis 1:1–2:25
The Flood – Read Genesis 6:1–8:22
The Tower of Babel – Read Genesis 11:1–9
Sodom and Gomorrah – Read Genesis 18:16–19:29

THE BOOK OF EXODUS

A STORY FOR ADVENTURE LOVERS THAT SHOWS GOD'S POWER AND FAITHFULNESS.

INTRODUCTION

What sort of films do you like watching? If you like nice, gentle, romantic films this might not be the book for you. If, on the other hand, you like your films fast moving and full of action and special effects, read on ...

GROUND COVERED

Exodus possibly tells the most exciting story in the Bible: the story of how God delivered His people from their slavery in Egypt and made an agreement with them to be their God for ever.

MAIN THEMES ||||||||||||||||||||||||||||||||||

Exodus can be split into two parts.

ESCAPE FROM EGYPT

Only the very best computer animators could do this part of the book justice if it were to be turned into a film – you'd need some serious special effects. A bush that's alight but doesn't burn might not be too taxing, but that's only the beginning. From there on it gets wild and crazy.

Walking sticks turn into snakes and back again; rivers run with blood; thousands of frogs and locusts swarm all through the land of Egypt. And in a great finale, the whole of the Israelite nation passes through the middle of the sea just before the waves come crashing back down on all the pursuing armies of Egypt.

Animating *Narnia* was child's play compared to that.

BUT WHAT ABOUT ME?

As we read this section of Exodus, we see not only the power of God but His love for His people. That's a comforting combination when we remember that Christians are now part of His chosen people.

'ME TARZAN, YOU JANE' OR 'I'M GOD, YOU ARE MY PEOPLE'

Boys often fantasise about what amazing feats they could perform to impress the girl they like. In a daydream, fighting off ten thugs and then carrying her away in your arms sounds quite reasonable, but of course things never quite turn out that way.

For God, though, it had worked. He'd really done the business in helping Israel escape from Egypt. And now that He'd saved them and got their attention, it was time for a marriage ceremony if they were going to live happily ever after.

The second part of the book of Exodus is, in effect, the marriage ceremony of the Old Testament. The wedding took place about three months after Israel left Egypt, at the foot of a mountain called Sinai. God appeared to the nation of Israel and through Moses made His promises to them. In return they agreed to keep all His laws.

Starting a pattern that runs all through the Old Testament, the Israelites almost immediately 'committed adultery' by worshipping another god in the form of a golden calf. Fortunately for them, and for all of us today, God is more faithful to His promises to us than we are to Him, and He took them back and continued to love them. Try to remember that next time you feel you've let God down.

INTERESTING BITS ||||||||||||||||||||||||||||||

Moses' early life – Read Exodus 2:1–4:31
The escape from Egypt – Read Exodus 7:1–14:31
Food and drink from God – Read Exodus 16:1–17:7
God on Mount Sinai – Read Exodus 19:1–25
The Ten Commandments – Read Exodus 20:1–17
The golden calf – Read Exodus 32:1–35

THE BOOK OF LEVITICUS

HOW TO LIVE WITH GOD WITHOUT GETTING STRUCK BY LIGHTNING.

INTRODUCTION

The police – do you love them or hate them? It tends to depend on the situation, doesn't it?

When you're running full tilt away from a gang who are trying to beat you up, that blue uniform would be the most welcome sight in the world. On the other hand, when you're enjoying a bit of winter fun throwing snowballs at passing cars, the appearance of that same blue uniform can make you feel physically sick.

That just about sums up our love–hate attitude to rules and laws. We love them when they're working for us, but hate them when they restrict us.

GROUND COVERED

Leviticus covers the laws that God gave to the ancient Israelites. The laws cover everything from food to sexuality, and from blood sacrifices to baldness. There are religious laws, and laws that focus on cleanness in food preparation or the quarantine of sick people – and others that deal with how to treat people who work for you, and the poor.

BUT WHAT ABOUT ME?

There is nothing more infuriating than living, even for a short space of time, with someone completely different to you. They stay up late; you like to get up early. You like your room to have a lived-in feel; they go crazy if a piece of clothing so much as hits the floor.

In those situations, sometimes the only way to avoid bloodshed is to create rules for living together, like the ones God gave to the Israelites. Fortunately for us, what Jesus did means that we can approach God without having to slaughter cute little animals!

INTERESTING BITS ||||||||||||||||||||||||

How offerings were made – Read Leviticus 1:1–17
The first priests are appointed – Read Leviticus 8:1–36
Charming rules about skin disease for acne sufferers
– Read Leviticus 13:1–46
Holidays for God's people – Read Leviticus 23:1–44
Rewards and punishments – Read Leviticus 26:1–39

THE BOOK OF
NUMBERS

INTRODUCTION

The Israelites were the biggest bunch of moaners in history. God kept them going round and round in circles till they learnt to shut their mouths and trust Him.

GROUND COVERED

Numbers picks up the story where Exodus left off. It is the sad story of Israel's forty years of wandering in the wilderness. (Phew, no more long lists of laws.)

So, why were they there for so long? It wasn't plan 'A', that's for certain. Plan 'A' was that they go in immediately and conquer the land that God had promised them, but they were scared of fighting and rebellious against Moses, their leader.

God took both of these things personally, so He made plan 'B': wander in the desert for forty years till all the cowardly rebellious people die off, then take a new generation into the promised land.

BUT WHAT ABOUT ME?

Some people give up too easily. Some friends will blow out a football game just because it's raining. Others will refuse to leave the house because their hair is not quite right.

Fortunately for us, God never gives up. We might blow it in a big way and think that we've messed up our lives forever, but as the story told in Numbers shows, God can always get us back on course.

INTERESTING BITS ||||||||||||||||||||||||||||

The people start moaning – Read Numbers 11:1–12:16
The spies go out spying – Read Numbers 13:1–33
The ground opens up – Read Numbers 16:1–40
Even Moses blows it – Read Numbers 20:1–13
Balaam and the talking donkey
– Read Numbers 22:1–24:25
A new leader is appointed – Read Numbers 27:12–23

THE BOOK OF
DEUTERONOMY

INTRODUCTION

I know this is a horrible thought, but have you ever
considered that some of the music you listen to on the
radio, and some of the albums you buy, might be by exactly
the same bands and singers that your parents liked when
they were teenagers?

What could be more uncool than buying a CD, then
coming back home to find that your dad's got the same
album on one of those old vinyl records? It's not just the
Beatles – other groups like the Rolling Stones, the Eagles,
even Eric Clapton, are all playing sell-out concerts by doing
reunion or farewell tours.

The book of Deuteronomy is Moses' final, farewell gig.
This is where he plays – or rather, speaks – some of the big
hit sermons/messages of the past from God, this time to a
whole new generation.

GROUND COVERED

Deuteronomy is a record of a number of sermons that
Moses preached to the Israelites just before he died, and
before they entered the promised land. In his talks he
covered all that God had spoken to him at Mount Sinai and
during the following years.

The messages needed to be given again because the
people entering the promised land were a completely new
generation to those who had left Egypt.

MAIN THEME

Some of the best teachers initially appear to be the most
harsh, unkind and strict. For the first few weeks of a term,
you live in fear and tell everyone that you've never had a

worse teacher. Then once they have established discipline and control they gradually relax, and you find that they're human after all (contrary to popular opinion, all teachers are human) and you really enjoy their class.

God sometimes appeared to the Israelites as hard and scary. He thundered on Mount Sinai, He set very high standards for the people to keep, and He killed those who rebelled against Him.

In Deuteronomy, Moses emphasises that God's love for the people is behind all His laws. God had chosen them to be His people not because they deserved it, but because He loved them. The laws were intended to make them happy and healthy. There were horrible consequences for disobeying God's laws, but these weren't punishment as such, just the natural results of not following God's advice.

BUT WHAT ABOUT ME?

It's easy as a Christian teen to focus on the 'don'ts' of Christianity. Sometimes it can seem as if all the fun things our friends do are off limits for us.

Deuteronomy teaches us an important lesson. God is not a killjoy, or an uninformed oldie who doesn't understand what life is like for young people today. He is our perfectly loving and perfectly wise heavenly Father whose laws can keep us safe and happy.

DEUTERONOMY

INTERESTING BITS ||||||||||||||||||||||||||

Love God and He will help you – Read Deuteronomy 6:1–25
God chose you because He loves you
– Read Deuteronomy 7:7–16
How to treat neighbours who are poor
– Read Deuteronomy 15:7–11
The results of obeying or disobeying
– Read Deuteronomy 28:1–68
The death of Moses – Read Deuteronomy 32:48–52; 34:1–12

50

THE **HISTORICAL** BOOKS

GENERAL INTRODUCTION

WHAT ARE THEY?

Do you prefer cross country or track running? Personally, I'd choose a jog through the park any day of the week. I'm afraid I get bored just going round and round in circles. Running is hard enough work as it is. I need at least to feel that I'm getting somewhere.

Most of the other religions of the world view history as 'cyclical' – like going round and round a track without ever actually getting anywhere. But as Christians we believe that history is 'linear' – it is progressing towards a fixed point. God has a purpose and a plan that He is working out in the world, and one day will come the end of time and the beginning of a new heaven and a new earth.

This group of Old Testament books tells the history of the nation of Israel from the time they first entered the promised land through to their return from captivity, which is where the Old Testament finishes.

SO WHY DID GOD BOTHER TO INCLUDE HISTORY BOOKS IN THE BIBLE?

Do you know what an 'oxymoron' is? No, it's not a new treatment for spots, nor a new slang word for someone who is intellectually challenged. An 'oxymoron' is a phrase that at first seems to be contradictory – like thunderous silence, bitter sweet or happy Monday.

The books that we are looking at are often called 'prophetic history', which can seem like an oxymoron – isn't prophecy about the future, and history about the past?

What this really means is that these books were written not just as records of the past, but to show what God was doing and what His purpose was in all of the events that are recorded. These books were intended right from the moment they were written to teach us about God.

SO THEY'RE NOT REAL HISTORY THEN?

Some people think that because the purpose of the books was to teach people about God, they can't be trusted to be true like 'real' history books.

Mentioned at different points in the books are sources of information that the writers used to make sure that what they wrote was accurate. These sources included court records from the times of the kings, biographies that had been written about the great men and women (like one called the 'Acts of Solomon'), actual memoirs (almost like diaries) of people like Ezra and Nehemiah, and also collections of the sayings and teachings of prophets like Elijah and Elisha.

Ancient historians, like the writers of these books, were not as concerned with exact dates and orders of events as we are today. But there is no reason to suspect that they made up things that didn't happen, or that what we read isn't genuine history.

BUT WHAT ABOUT ME?

For me there is something uniquely exciting about a cricket test match. Minute by minute there may not be the same excitement level as basketball or football. In fact, it might actually be quite boring. But there is something about the grand scale of it – a game lasting five whole days, played nation against nation – that somehow sets it above other contests that are over in an hour.

The same is true of the historical books. The sheer scale of them – centuries of the history of a whole nation – allows us a glimpse of how big God is.

He's not like us. We work towards something next week, or possibly next month, and we have enough trouble arranging our own lives without bothering with anyone else's. God works through whole nations of the world, and over millennia, to achieve what He wants to. It's a bit of a cliché, but 'What a mighty God we serve!'

These books also include some of the most exciting and interesting stories in the whole of the Bible – so grab a mug of hot chocolate, throw the cat out of your favourite armchair and settle down for a good read.

THE BOOK OF
JOSHUA

A BOOK FOR PEOPLE FACING CHALLENGING SITUATIONS.

INTRODUCTION

Out of the frying pan and into the fire. I hate those situations. You've escaped one disaster by running back home to collect forgotten homework. Then you realise that you're in even deeper trouble – you're late for school.

The Israelites' whole lives seemed to be like that.

They escape as slaves from Egypt, only to wander in the wilderness for forty years. Then when that's finally over, it's time to start fighting their way into the promised land.

GROUND COVERED

I used to love war stories, in books, comics or films. (I'm sorry – it's a boy thing.) I wasn't much into reading the Bible at the time, but had I been I'd have loved the book of Joshua.

It tells about the military conquest of the land of Canaan by the Israelites. They were led by Joshua, a brilliant soldier and leader, as well as a man of God.

The first half of the book is full of spies, battles, strategy, heroics and times when God did miracles for His people. The second part of the book mostly concerns the way the land was divided among the twelve tribes of Israel.

MAIN THEME ||||||||||||||||||||||||||||||||||

They say that elephants never forget.
God never forgets either. Hundreds of years before Joshua, God had made two promises. One to Abraham – that one day his descendants would live in Canaan. The other to the cruel and evil people who lived there – that He would punish them for their evil ways (human sacrifice, murder of babies and religious prostitution).

In Joshua both promises are kept at once.

BUT WHAT ABOUT ME?

The Israelites could have lived forever in a wilderness that no other nation wanted, but they would never have seen God fighting for them, or experienced God's best plan for them.

The Christian life is not easy. Sometimes we have to step out into difficult situations before God can begin to help us.

⭐ INTERESTING BITS ||||||||||||||||||||||||||||

Undercover spying mission – Read Joshua 2:1–24
The famous battle of Jericho – Read Joshua 6:1–27
The sun stands still – Read Joshua 10:1–14
Joshua's final words of challenge – Read Joshua 23:1–24:27

THE BOOK OF
THE JUDGES

A BOOK FOR THOSE OF US WHO MAKE THE SAME
MISTAKES AGAIN AND AGAIN.

INTRODUCTION

Vicious circles are not related to slime, or swamp men,
or any of the other evil, flesh-eating characters out of
countless Hollywood B-movies. They are bad patterns that
keep repeating themselves, just like the one the Israelites
find themselves trapped in here.

GROUND COVERED

In my humble opinion, weekdays are nothing more than
bridges between weekends – when life is *really* lived.

The book of Judges bridges the time between Israel
conquering the land, and crowning a king. The vicious
circle was one of forgetting God ... getting into trouble ...
screaming to God for help ... God anointing a Judge to save
the people ... times of peace ... forgetting God ... getting into
trouble ... and so on.

MAIN THEME ||||||||||||||||||||||||||||||||

Who do you think would still love you if you made the same stupid mistake for the billionth time? Possibly only your mother!

God shows His incredible patience with His people in the book of Judges. He saves them from their own stupidity time and time again.

BUT WHAT ABOUT ME?

We can all see ourselves in the pattern above. In good times we forget God and go off to do our own thing. In rough times we remember Him and ask for help. Then we forget about Him again.

God is so patient with us. We must never be afraid to go to Him for help, but if we can break out of the vicious circle we'll be much better off.

CENTRAL CHARACTERS

These Judges didn't wear white wigs and hand down criminal sentences. They were warriors whom God anointed to unite the Israelites and defeat their enemies.

WHERE TO FIND THEM
The first Judge sets the pattern – Read Judges 3:7-11
Deborah the woman Judge – Read Judges 4-5
Gideon the coward becomes Judge Dredd
– Read Judges 6-8
Samson the Judge – Read Judges 13-16

THE STORY OF
RUTH

Ruth is a love story from the time of the Judges.
(About time too after all the war and battle that's
been going on recently!)
Read it – it's only four chapters long.

THE BOOKS OF
1 AND 2 SAMUEL

INTRODUCTION

'We don't have anyone to put on the front of *Hello*
magazine,' they cried. 'We need a royal family!'
   In the time of 1 and 2 Samuel, the cry from the people
was for a king.

GROUND COVERED

The two books cover the reigns of the first two kings of
Israel, both of whom were appointed by God through
Samuel, the last of the Judges.
   The first, Saul, showed all that could be wrong with a
king. The second, David, made many mistakes, but he was
the greatest ever ruler of Israel. (He must be impressive –
Richard Gere played him in a film.)

MAIN THEME

God knew a king was not what Israel needed, but it might work if the king worked under God's ultimate rule, as God's chosen leader.

In the first part of David's reign, the country enjoyed incredible success in war and every other way because he served God. However, when the king went wrong and sinned and rebelled, it affected the whole nation.

BUT WHAT ABOUT ME?

Here's a little brainteaser for you. Would you rather God gave you what you want, or what you need?

Sometimes God gives us what we ask for, and not what He knows we need (like giving the Israelites a king). At these times we often start off happy and end up sad (the Israelites soon came to resent their kings). Other times, God refuses what we ask for but gives us what He knows we need. These times are better – we may start sad but we finish happy, because God knows best.

CENTRAL CHARACTERS

Samuel, last Judge and kingmaker – Early life
– Read 1 Samuel 1:1–3:21, then through the rest of
  1 Samuel
Saul, first king of Israel – Becomes king
– Read 1 Samuel 9:1–10:27 and elsewhere
David, great king of Israel (see below)

INTERESTING BITS

The people demand a king – Read 1 Samuel 8:1–22
David fights the giant – Read 1 Samuel 17:1–58
David and Jonathan – Read 1 Samuel 18:1–20:42
David becomes king of all Israel – Read 2 Samuel 5:1–5
God's promise to David – Read 2 Samuel 7:1–29
David and Bathsheba – Read 2 Samuel 11:1–12:25

THE BOOKS OF
1 AND 2 KINGS

BOOKS FOR THOSE WHO ARE WILLING TO SWIM AGAINST
THE CURRENT.

INTRODUCTION

Few things in life are as fun as riding a bike fast downhill.
The wind rushes past, there's no effort and the danger gets
the adrenaline pumping.

1 and 2 Kings see Israel rushing faster and faster
downhill on a bike without brakes. It's just a matter of time
before there's an almighty crash.

GROUND COVERED

1 and 2 Kings cover about 400 years of Israel's history, all
of it downhill. From the peak of David and Solomon's reign,
past the sad split into the two separate nations of Israel
and Judah, and then ever down to the bottom of the hill and
a big and painful crash.

Within 150 years of each other, both of the nations were
conquered and the survivors carried off into captivity.

MAIN THEME

Only a stupid teacher would hand out detentions without
explaining what they are for. If you don't understand why
you're being punished, you can't learn.

1 and 2 Kings were probably compiled from earlier
accounts while the people were in exile – God's punishment
for their sin. The books showed that God hadn't let the
people down – the people had walked away from God. The
hope of the writers was that if everyone understood this,
they wouldn't make the same mistakes next time.

BUT WHAT ABOUT ME?

As you read 1 and 2 Kings, look for the outstanding kings and prophets who were prepared to go against the flow and stand for God in their day. God is still looking for people with the guts to take a stand for Him and not just take the easy options.

CENTRAL CHARACTERS

Solomon, the richest king – Read 1 Kings 1:28–11:43
Ahab and his wife Jezebel, the worst of the worst, and the pattern for all the bad kings who followed – Read 1 Kings 16:29–22:40

Elijah and Elisha, two great prophets who followed God even when everyone else was doing their own thing – Read 1 Kings 17:1–21:28; 2 Kings 1:1–13:21

INTERESTING BITS

Solomon's wisdom – Read 1 Kings 3:1–28; 4:29–34
The nation is split – Read 1 Kings 12:1–33
Joash the youngest king – Read 2 Kings 11:1–12:21
Josiah, at last a good king – Read 2 Kings 22:1–23:30
The northern kingdom destroyed - Read 2 Kings 17:1–18
Judah is also destroyed – Read 2 Kings 25:1–21

THE BOOKS OF
1 AND 2 CHRONICLES

BOOKS FOR PEOPLE WHO NEVER GIVE UP.

INTRODUCTION

I've yet to hear a real die-hard football fan complain about seeing replays of a great goal seven times. That's because each camera angle shows you something different about the player's skills.

Lots of people do complain that 1 and 2 Chronicles is just a replay of Kings. Well, it is, but from a different camera angle, so we learn a lot more about what was going on.

GROUND COVERED

Historically, the book of Chronicles covers the same period as 1 and 2 Kings, but it focuses on different things.

Good times instead of bad times.

Kings descended from David instead of all the kings.

The southern kingdom of Judah instead of both kingdoms.

The Temple and worship, instead of false gods and idolatry.

MAIN THEME

Eventually some people from the nation of Judah returned home from their long captivity. As they tried to rebuild their homes and their nation, it was important that they knew why they had failed in the past, and be encouraged about the future.

The most important lesson for them to learn was that the success of their nation depended absolutely on the way the people related to God. When they followed Him, things went well. When they left Him behind, or worshipped other gods, things went downhill fast.

BUT WHAT ABOUT ME?

A writer called G.K. Chesterton, who constantly struggled to be on time, once said that the only way to catch a train is to miss the one before it. Others have said that you've only really failed once you've given up trying.

Failures are OK provided you get up and try again. That's a great attitude to have in our lives, especially in our relationship with God.

INTERESTING BITS ||||||||||||||||||||||||||

The first people to return – Read 1 Chronicles 9:1–34
David's mighty army – Read 1 Chronicles 11–12
David's prayer for the Temple – Read 1 Chronicles 29:10–20
God comes to the Temple – Read 2 Chronicles 7:1–22
God defends Jerusalem – Read 2 Chronicles 32:1–23

THE BOOK OF
EZRA

A BOOK ALL ABOUT BALANCE.

INTRODUCTION

Did you ever watch the old Disney film *Swiss Family Robinson*? The family shipwrecked on a desert island had to learn to survive without any of the conveniences they were used to, as well as fight off all sorts of enemies. Just like the Jews of Ezra returning to a destroyed city.

GROUND COVERED

Ezra tells the story of the Jews who were allowed home to Jerusalem after their time in captivity. They had to learn to survive, not only physically but spiritually.

◉ MAIN THEME ||||||||||||||||||||||||||||||||||||||

Here's an easy question: If you add dirty water to clean water, is the bucket full of clean or dirty water? Dirty, obviously.

Ezra knew it would be the same with the Jews returning to Jerusalem. If they mixed with the evil, ungodly people living around Jerusalem they would end up dirty too. So he commanded the people to keep God's laws, confess their sin, and not mix too much with the surrounding people.

BUT WHAT ABOUT ME?

I have always wanted to try tightrope walking – though preferably a few feet rather than a few hundred feet off the ground.

As Christians, we are called to walk a sort of tightrope. Since we have God's Spirit to empower us, we don't have to steer as far clear of non-Christians as the Jews. But we *are* called to find the right balance of being *in* the world, among non-Christians, but not *of* it (or not quite like non-Christians). That's a balancing act to work on for the rest of our lives.

EZRA

CENTRAL CHARACTERS

Cyrus, Darius, Xerxes and Artaxerxes were all rulers in the lands to which the Israelites had been taken captive – Read Ezra 1–6

Ezra was a great scholar and teacher, and a direct descendant of the high priests in the time of the kings – Read Ezra 7–10

THE BOOK OF
NEHEMIAH

A BOOK THAT PROVES IT'S POSSIBLE TO WIN AGAINST THE
ODDS – ESPECIALLY IF YOU'VE GOT GOD ON YOUR SIDE!

INTRODUCTION

In ancient times, a city without walls was about as useful as
a convertible security van. Imagine: out comes the sun, up
goes the temperature, down comes the hood, and bye-bye
to all those nice bags full of money.

Unwalled cities were vulnerable to neighbouring tribes
who would simply march right in and head off with people's
TVs, PCs and lots of other good stuff. Nehemiah is all about
the rebuilding of Jerusalem's walls.

GROUND COVERED

One day you might have to choose between a job where you'll
get paid lots of money, and one that you believe is important.

Nehemiah had a safe and probably well-paid job, serving
the king of Persia. When he heard that those who had
returned to Jerusalem had not yet rebuilt the walls of the
city, he knew he was the man to do the job, but it would
mean giving up a lot.

MAIN THEME ||||||||||||||||||||||||||||||

A friend of mine called 'Greenie' (nothing at all to do with
his nose) was the full back on our rugby team. The problem
was that he was short, skinny and desperately taking
growth hormones. But he was also totally fearless. Over-
confident players would run straight at 'Greenie', certain of
a try – and then be flattened by the little guy.

As humans, we love the underdog – the person who
beats all the odds. In Nehemiah we watch the Jews as, with
God's help, they beat all the odds.

BUT WHAT ABOUT ME?

Nehemiah never gave up. There were times when he was being threatened, and his nice safe job serving the king must have seemed like a dream – but he kept going.

Persistence is a trait that God likes and can work with. Next time you hit a wall, keep going, keep pushing, and let God help you through.

INTERESTING BITS |||||||||||||||||||||||||||||

Nehemiah decides to go to Jerusalem
– Read Nehemiah 1:1–2:10
Keeping on in spite of threats – Read Nehemiah 4:1–23
The people hear a sermon from Ezra
– Read Nehemiah 8:1–18
Celebrations for the completed walls
– Read Nehemiah 12:27–43

THE BOOK OF
ESTHER

INTRODUCTION

Do you prefer your heroines to be all-action types, like Princess Leia in *Star Wars* and Lara Croft in *Tomb Raider*, or the more traditional feminine type? Although Esther is very beautiful, this is no love story. Esther ends up saving the whole nation of Israel through her bravery.

GROUND COVERED

The story told in Esther takes place at the same time as the events in the books of Ezra and Nehemiah. It's the story of a beautiful young Jewish girl who is chosen to be one of the queens of the Persian king Xerxes.

While she is queen, a plot is hatched to destroy all of the Jewish people. Fortunately for them, Esther is in the right place at the right time, and with the encouragement of the right relative, to stop the evil plan.

It still takes plenty of guts on her part, though, as even a queen could be killed for entering the king's presence unannounced, let alone trying to change his mind.

MAIN THEME |||||||||||||||||||||||||||||||||

Amazingly – this *is*, after all, the Bible – God is not mentioned in the whole book of Esther. That doesn't mean that He isn't working behind the scenes, though.

It is typical of Satan that at a critical time like this, when the exiles are being allowed back to Jerusalem and the Temple is being built, he tries to sneak a cruel plan in behind God's back. It doesn't work, though, thanks to Esther and Mordecai.

CENTRAL CHARACTERS

King Xerxes, the incredibly powerful king of Persia.
Esther, his young and beautiful Jewish queen.
Haman, the evil schemer who wants to kill off the Jews.
Mordecai, Esther's brave cousin who uncovers the plot.

INTERESTING BITS |||||||||||||||||||||||||||

It's an exciting story, so get a good modern translation and just read it!

THE BOOKS OF **POETRY** AND **WISDOM**

GENERAL INTRODUCTION

Why are these books grouped together? The Jewish people split their Old Testament into three sections. The law, the prophets (which include the history books) and the writings. The five books that we are looking at now all come from the 'writings' section of the Jewish Old Testament.

WHAT IS POETRY?

'I wouldn't be caught dead with a poem in my hand. That's for snobs and weirdos – not for me!'

When we talk like that, we're probably only thinking of a particular type of poetry, and we forget that song lyrics, limericks ('There was an old man from ...') and nursery rhymes ('Hey diddle diddle') are poetry as well.

The ancient Israelites used poetry much more than we do today, and all of the books in this section use some. The intention was to make the books more memorable, more entertaining, and more full of feeling than normal writing often allows. Fortunately, this kind of poetry didn't rely too much on rhymes or precise rhythms, so we can still understand it even when translated.

WHAT DOES WISDOM MEAN?

'It takes more than a few exams to make you wise. Real wisdom only comes to older people who have experienced life.'

This was the thinking in Old Testament times. Grey hair was considered the greatest sign of wisdom, because back then you must have done something right just to have lived that long. For this reason, the sayings and teachings of the wise were treasured and written down, and then taught to young people like a sort of textbook on how to live life.

There are two types of wisdom writing in the books we are looking at: 'proverbs' (in the book of Proverbs – makes sense that), and 'reflection' (see Job and Ecclesiastes).

Proverbs are short, sharp, often funny sayings with a point to make.

Reflective wisdom is deeper, more thoughtful, and often takes the form of a conversation (Job) or a long speech (Ecclesiastes).

CENTRAL CHARACTERS

David

Psalms is the longest book in the Bible, and the main man behind it is David. His love of worshipping God through music is legendary, and it is thought that he brought together what might have been the world's first orchestra to aid the people in their worship.

After his death, music became a very important part of worshipping God in the Temple. So even though David couldn't possibly have written most of the Psalms, his influence was very important.

Solomon

When it comes to wisdom, Solomon is the man. The Bible shows that his remarkable wisdom was a gift from God, but he made the most of his natural gift by some serious studying.

When he ruled, Israel was known as a centre of science and thought, and many wise men travelled there to teach and to learn. Solomon and others learnt all they could from the wise men from around the world, then improved on this knowledge by applying to it the special things that God had taught them.

Solomon's name is sometimes attached as author to all three of the wisdom books. At the very least, we know that he wrote some of the Proverbs and possibly Ecclesiastes.

THE BOOK OF
JOB

A BOOK FOR THOSE WHO ARE SUFFERING.

INTRODUCTION

What's the worst thing that has ever happened to you? Is it failing an exam, waking up with a terrible case of zits, or something rather more serious?

It can be very confusing to believe in a good and all powerful God, and then have to suffer or watch other innocent people suffer. That is not a new problem, and it is one that is faced head-on in the book of Job.

GROUND COVERED

There are bad days (Mondays are always bad days), very bad days (drizzly Mondays when you haven't done your homework) and very, *very* bad days (we're talking 'nothing goes right, even the cat hates you' sort of days), but few of us have ever experienced bad days like Job.

Job was a very good and very wealthy man. Suddenly everything went wrong for him – he lost his whole family, all of his wealth was wiped out and he himself became covered in ugly and painful boils.

Some of Job's friends were convinced that he must have done something very wrong to have caused all this, but he knew he was innocent.

MAIN THEME ||||||||||||||||||||||||||||||

Right at the end of the book, Job is privileged to speak to God. God does not answer his questions as to why these things happened. He simply shows His greatness and His justice.

In the end, Job realises that what is important is not knowing the answer, but knowing God.

BUT WHAT ABOUT ME?

As you read through Job you will see the impossibility of trying to understand the cause of every unfair thing that happens in the world. Like Job, we need to learn that our quest must be to find God, not to find an answer. The more we know God, the more certain we can be that He will work things out fairly in the end.

INTERESTING BITS ||||||||||||||||||||||||

The start of all the trouble – Read Job 1:1–2:10
The Lord speaks to Job – Read Job 38:1–40:2
Are these monsters dinosaurs? – Read Job 40:15–41:34
Happy ever after – Read Job 42:10–17

THE BOOK OF
PROVERBS

A BOOK OF TIMELESS ADVICE FOR LIVING LIFE.

INTRODUCTION

Some people are just naturally practical. At school they can be heard saying: 'As if I'm ever going to need to know who was king of England in 1066 – I can always find it on *Wikipedia* anyway.'

If they wanted to read the Bible, Proverbs would be their book.

GROUND COVERED

Some so-called geniuses can't even explain how to use the lavatory without taking two hours and using data projectors and PowerPoints.

Not so the writers of Proverbs. This book is a collection of the teachings of a number of wise men, boiled down to the smallest possible units. Short sayings summarise their teaching and make the point better than many long sermons. What's more, you can remember them afterwards too.

These short sayings are called proverbs, and they contain sound, practical advice on many aspects of life.

MAIN THEME

If you're building, you need foundations. If you don't have a foundation, then your architectural masterpiece is going to be as flat as a pancake in a very short space of time.

The wise men of Proverbs knew that wisdom also requires a firm foundation. The foundation that they chose was the 'fear of the Lord'. It was only if you already understood something of God and respected (feared) Him that you would benefit from their teaching.

 BUT WHAT ABOUT ME?

Advice on chariot racing or how to ride a camel, wouldn't be of much use to us today. Fortunately, that is not what the proverbs are all about. Instead, they deal with timeless themes such as honesty, gossip, pride, loyalty and greed.

⭐ **INTERESTING BITS** |||||||||||||||||||||||||||

A FEW PEACHES
The firm foundation – Read Proverbs 9:10
When is a beautiful woman like a pig? – Read Proverbs 11:22

SOME MORE PLUMS
Money often sprouts wings and flies off
– Read Proverbs 23:4–5
An honest answer is like a kiss on the lips
– Read Proverbs 24:26

THE BOOK OF
PSALMS

INTRODUCTION

Can you imagine Christians singing today's worship songs in 2,000 years' time? They'll be in their spacesuits up on Mars singing 'My Jesus, my Saviour' through their headset microphones!

I wonder if the writers of the book of Psalms knew that it would be around for thousands of years and still used as a songbook by Christians and Jews alike.

GROUND COVERED

If you went down the road to the local music store and asked for a single CD that brought together classical, dance, drum and bass, soul and indie music, the assistant would look at you rather strangely.

Yet in the book of Psalms the 150 songs of worship to God are about as different as the music listed above. There are loud songs to be sung by massed choirs and big orchestras. There are quiet meditative songs to be sung by one person to God. There are sad songs, as well as songs of celebration.

MAIN THEMES ||||||||||||||||||||||||||||||||||

GOD AND LIFE

It is impossible to pick one main theme out of the Psalms – they deal with every aspect of life, and every possible emotion and feeling towards God. The psalm writers rightly assume that God is involved in all of these situations and wants to be part of every area of our lives.

THIS IS A LYRIC, NOT A THEOLOGY ESSAY

What is the dumbest song lyric you've ever heard? There are some stupid ones aren't there? But that doesn't always mean that the songs aren't good, or that you don't understand what the songwriter means. When you listen to a song you don't expect to come away with a deeper understanding of nuclear physics, but you do expect to feel something.

In the same way, the writers of the Psalms were focusing on their feelings towards God rather than theology. When the writers cry out for their enemies' babies to be dashed against rocks, this is obviously not something that God would approve of, but it is in the Psalms because it shows honestly how people felt.

When you read the Psalms, be aware that these are song lyrics and not theology – don't copy everything that is said and done!

JESUS IN THE PSALMS

Royal Psalms like 2, 72 and 110 speak of a king and spiritual leader so perfect that only Jesus could possibly match up. Other Psalms, particularly 22, describe the suffering that Jesus endured. As you read the Psalms, look out for the shadow of Jesus just behind the words that you are reading, even though they were written hundreds of years before Jesus came to earth.

 BUT WHAT ABOUT ME?

I hate those tongue-tied situations when you just don't know what to say. You stand there with your mouth opening and closing stupidly, with no words coming out.

The Psalms, though, can help us express ourselves to God. Not only can we look for a psalm that fits what we want to say – and believe me, there's one for every occasion – the Psalms also show us that it is OK to tell God everything. If you're angry, tell Him. If you're sad, explain. If you're confused, lay it all out honestly.

⭐ **INTERESTING BITS – SIX OF THE BEST** ‖‖‖‖‖‖

If you want to try some psalms, start here:

The world famous 'The Lord is my shepherd'
– Read Psalm 23

When you've messed up bad, try this – Read Psalm 51

When life seems frightening, look here – Read Psalm 91

The longest chapter in the Bible, but good – Read Psalm 119

God knows and loves you – Read Psalm 139

The last psalm needs major decibels to work right
– Read Psalm 150

THE BOOK OF
ECCLESIASTES

A BOOK THAT'S NOT AFRAID TO LOOK AT THE DOWNSIDE OF LIFE.

INTRODUCTION

According to the media, the younger generations are cynical and hopeless, we trust nothing and no one. That attitude is nothing new – the author of Ecclesiastes (probably Solomon) felt the same way.

GROUND COVERED

If you had money to burn, a kingdom to rule and hundreds of beautiful wives to keep you company, would you be happy? 'Of course!' you cry!

Well, King Solomon wrote a book that focuses on all the unfairness, the cruelty and the pointlessness in the world. Nowhere does he find anything that brings true happiness – not hard work, or money, or goodness. Even looking for fun gets boring after a time.

MAIN THEME

So, what's such a pessimistic book doing in the Bible? The truth is that much of what the writer outlines is true. Life is terribly unfair – what did you and I do to deserve to be born in a wealthy country? Also, none of the things he talks about can make anyone truly happy.

But we must view the book of Ecclesiastes alongside the rest of the Bible. Then we can see that God's presence makes life worth living, and His justice puts all the unfairness of life into a new perspective.

BUT WHAT ABOUT ME?

Sometimes Christians are accused of looking at the world through rose-coloured spectacles – pretending that life is easier and fairer than it really is. It is possible to enjoy our relationship with God and our hope of heaven so much that we forget other people's difficulties and pain. A quick reading of the book of Ecclesiastes is good medicine for this problem.

INTERESTING BITS ||||||||||||||||||||||||

Setting the tone (what's the point?)
– Read Ecclesiastes 1:1–11
Is there a time for everything?
– Read Ecclesiastes 3:1–8
Face difficult times with friends
– Read Ecclesiastes 4:9–12
Start serving God while you're young
– Read Ecclesiastes 11:7–12:5
A final word of advice – Read Ecclesiastes 12:9–14

THE BOOK OF
THE SONG OF SOLOMON

A BOOK THAT GIVES A 'GOD'S-EYE-VIEW' OF SEX.

INTRODUCTION

There are two kinds of romantics – those who admit they're romantics, and those who hide it. Generally the members of the first group are girls, and the second are boys. Yes, boys are romantics too, they just hide it. The fact that this book is in the Bible proves that God is a romantic too.

GROUND COVERED

Reading the Song of Solomon is like reading somebody else's love letters – naughty but nice.

It is a steamy collection of songs or poems sung by two lovers to one another. They sing of their attraction to each other, their physical desire for one another's bodies and their longing to be together. The man could have been King Solomon, and the woman was likely to have been a beautiful young girl whom he added to his collection of wives.

MAIN THEME

Many people have tried very hard over the centuries to make this book mean something they thought was really spiritual, but it's still not totally clear whether this Bible book is simply about sexual love or whether it all has hidden deep spiritual meaning.

BUT WHAT ABOUT ME?

We live in a sex-crazed world. Advertisers use sex to sell everything from diamonds to washing machines – and what could be less sexy than a washing machine?

This book helps us to put sex in its proper place. It is a wonderful gift that God finds beautiful, but it belongs only within marriage – not on billboards, or in films, or in one night stands. These things actually make sex valueless, and not the precious gift that God made it.

INTERESTING BITS

The man's description of his bride
– Read Song of Solomon 4:1–7
The woman describes her husband
– Read Song of Solomon 5:10–16

THE OLD TESTAMENT PROPHETS

GENERAL INTRODUCTION

WHO WERE THEY?

Walking down a dark street late at night, on your way home from a party, you see a group walking towards you that makes you want to cross to the other side of the street – just to be on the safe side.

If you saw the Old Testament prophets walking towards you, you would probably want to do the same thing. These were real characters, men called by God from various walks of life to be His spokesmen. It wasn't an easy, popular or a safe task, and you had to be a certain type of man.

WOULD YOU LIKE A JOB AS A PROPHET?

PROPHET
REQUIRED QUALIFICATIONS:

ACADEMIC BACKGROUND

None
Farmers, priests,
minor royals,
all welcome

CHARACTER
- Must be strong independent type
- Must be able to stand up under threats
- Must be willing to die for what you believe
- Must be holy enough to be close to God
- Must not care what other people think of you

STILL THINK YOU'RE THE PERSON FOR THE JOB? THEN READ ON.>>

WHAT WILL I HAVE TO SAY?
'Fortune tellers don't get death threats,' you might be saying. 'The man who does the horoscopes on morning TV is a nice, friendly guy. I can't imagine him being hated and threatened. What did the Old Testament prophets do to be so unpopular?'

The predictions of the prophets weren't the nice comfortable 'you'll meet a tall dark stranger' of the horoscopes, or the intriguingly weird predictions of modern doomsayers. Instead, they were strong words from God to the people of the time, generally calling them to change their ways and return to Him.

HOW WILL I KNOW WHAT TO SAY?
When you know someone really well, you know what really winds them up and what really makes them happy. If you wanted to be a prophet you had to have that sort of close relationship with God. The prophets knew and understood Him better than anyone else alive in their times.

They understood how God expected things to be, and God spoke to them about what was wrong in their societies. Their prophecies weren't half-mad ramblings but carefully constructed sermons and messages that could be preached with great power.

BUT DO I GET TO PREDICT THE FUTURE?

You'd better believe it, but not as often as you might think. God is Lord of all of history, and when it suits His purposes it is not a problem for Him to reveal what is going to happen to His spokesmen, the prophets.

But He doesn't do it just for the sake of it or to give people a thrill. No, He only allows His prophets to predict future events for a purpose. Normally this is either to warn the nation of something bad about to happen or to give them hope after something bad has happened.

STUDYING THE OLD TESTAMENT PROPHETS IN THIS BOOK

It's a crazy world we live in. Did you know that perfectly boring, respectable academics in our universities are now saying that time travel is, at least theoretically, possible? They have absolutely no idea how – although they're certain it won't be in an old blue police telephone box – but they think it could be done. I can't wait!

When we read the words of the Old Testament prophets, we are travelling 2,500 years back in time. This has advantages and disadvantages. Positively we can see how good their predictions were, but negatively we find it hard to understand the relevance of what they had to say when we know nothing about the situation at the time.

In the next chapters we have pulled together groups of prophets who prophesied at approximately the same time about the same events. This means that we will not follow exactly the same order as the Bible, but hopefully this will make what they had to say easier to understand.

ISAIAH, MICAH, AMOS AND HOSEA

PROPHETS BEFORE THE FALL OF THE NORTHERN KINGDOM.

THE TIMES THEY LIVED IN

ENEMIES

There were some big bullies knocking around Israel's neck of the woods at this time – the Assyrians. Their home and empire was in the north, but they had the muscle to control the lands to the south as well, including the northern and southern kingdoms of Israel.

They were the superpower of the time, and they knew it. They just loved throwing their weight around.

POLITICS

The big question with bullies is deciding when to stand up to them. 'Is today the day to risk losing my teeth, or should I just give them my lunch money again?' was roughly the decision the kings of the northern kingdom had to make.

After a period of paying up their lunch money, they made the brave but foolish decision to stand up to the Assyrians. Faster than you could say 'Not this time, matey', the bullies had swept down from the north like an avalanche and the northern kingdom was flat like a pancake.

LIFESTYLES

Strangely enough, right up to the very moment the big Assyrian Doc Marten boot descended on top of them, plenty of the inhabitants of the northern kingdom were on a 'nice little earner'.

It might not be fun being controlled by another nation, but it did help trade along. The rich people were getting richer by the minute and were practically fighting each other over nice locations to build themselves big 'Beverly Hills style' mansions.

At the same time, the poor people were suffering. While this didn't bother the rich people, it bothered God and His prophets – a lot!

RELIGION

'If it feels good, do it' was the normal attitude to religion at this time.

The people of the northern kingdom thought religion was just an excuse for big national holidays every once in a while.

They would mix in any parts of other foreign religions that seemed like fun, and just have a bit of a laugh. This made God very angry.

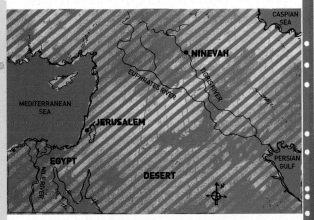

MAP OF THE ASSYRIAN EMPIRE

THE PROPHET
ISAIAH

A BOOK FOR THOSE WHO NEED HOPE FOR THE FUTURE.

THE MAN
Isaiah was probably a minor member of the royal family,
and so he could have enjoyed a wealthy and comfortable life
with his wife, who was also a prophetess, and his two sons.
You know: opening a village fête here and a library there.

Instead, he spent his life speaking God's (often unpopular)
words to his nation. Eventually he was killed for his truthful-
ness when the wicked King Manasseh had him sawn in two.

HIS MESSAGE
I love a good sandwich – fresh bread, pickle, anchovies and
lots of strawberry jam – only joking about the jam!

Isaiah's message was a bit like a strange sandwich. The
first bit of bread (chapters 1–35) was very bitter for the
people to eat, because Isaiah prophesies the judgment that
is coming.

The bottom bit of bread (chapters 40–66) was really
sweet, more like a cake than bread, because Isaiah talks of
hope for the future after the judgment.

The bit in the middle (chapters 36–39) tells how God
delivered King Hezekiah and the city of Jerusalem from the
mighty Assyrian king Sennacherib.

BUT WHAT ABOUT ME?
So many things in life start off exciting and then just fizzle
out with time. Just think of relationships, your favourite
football team's season and television series. With God,
things always get better and more exciting towards the end.

We see this in the book of Isaiah. With God, judgment is

never the end of the story, only the beginning. As one of the Psalms says: 'For his anger lasts only a moment, but his favour lasts a lifetime' (Psalm 30:5).

Remember this fact about God when you next feel depressed with life, or when you feel you've failed Him. With God, the best is always yet to come!

⭐ INTERESTING BITS ||||||||||||||||||||||||||||||

The story of Isaiah's call – Read Isaiah 6:1–13
A popular reading for Christmas – Read Isaiah 9:1–7
A picture of the end of the world – Read Isaiah 24:1–23
The story of the siege of Jerusalem – Read Isaiah 35–39
Prophetic description of Jesus – Read Isaiah 52:13–53:12
Jesus preached from this passage – Read Isaiah 61:1–2

THE PROPHET
MICAH

A BOOK ABOUT WHAT MAKES GOD HAPPY.

THE MAN

Micah was as poor and unconnected as Isaiah was rich and well bred. This poor country bumpkin bravely prophesied what God was going to do to the arrogant and wealthy capital cities of the two kingdoms of Israel.

HIS MESSAGE

The Israelites had worked out what they thought was a wonderful wheeze: 'Look, lads, I've got a plan. You know that when we sin we offer sacrifices to God to pay for it, right? Well, why don't we sin as much as we possibly can – really enjoy ourselves – then offer God lots and lots of sacrifices to pay for it? Then everyone's happy. God gets lots of sacrifices, and we get to do what we like!'

The false prophets who got paid commission on the number of animals sacrificed said this was fine, but God made His real feelings known through Micah.

God wasn't interested in the big, religious shows the people put on, especially when they began to offer human sacrifices. He was interested in the way they lived their normal lives, and how they treated Him and other people.

 ## BUT WHAT ABOUT ME?

No doubt we've all tried something similar to the plan above. We think we can live how we like all week so long as we ask God to forgive us in church on Sunday.

But God's not interested in how we look when we worship on Sunday, or in how spiritual we sound when we pray. He's interested in how we live every day of the week.

⭐ INTERESTING BITS ||||||||||||||||||||||||||
Read Micah 6:6–8

THE PROPHET
AMOS

A BOOK TO REMIND US NEVER TO FORGET LESS FORTUNATE PEOPLE.

THE MAN

Imagine being told by God to stand outside the gates of the roughest school in town and preach to the toughest gangs coming out.

That was Amos's mission from God. He was just a quiet shepherd and gardener from the hills in the southern kingdom, but God sent him to preach in the religious centre of the bigger, badder northern kingdom.

HIS MESSAGE

There's nothing as helpful as a bit of flattery, and what Amos had to say was *nothing* like a bit of flattery. He started out by calling the wealthy women of Israel cows, and finished by telling them that they were going to be dragged away by their enemies on hooks (which was how the Assyrians led away their captives).

Amos focused on one of the many things that had made God angry with the northern kingdom – the way the rich treated the poor. They cheated them, they sold them bread at ridiculously high prices and they bribed judges to keep them quiet.

Amos prophesied that God was going to judge this cruelty, and he was right. Just twenty years later the Assyrians invaded and destroyed the whole land, taking all the wealthy people away into exile.

BUT WHAT ABOUT ME?

God cares about poor and suffering people. If we want to make Him angry, there's no better way than treating such people unfairly. If we want to be like Him we need to help people less fortunate than ourselves.

INTERESTING BITS

Read Amos 3:13–4:5
Read Amos 5:11–15

THE PROPHET
HOSEA

A BOOK THAT SHOWS THAT NO ONE LOVES YOU LIKE GOD LOVES YOU.

THE MAN

Hosea was told by God to marry a prostitute. I'll repeat that in case you missed it – a *prostitute*. Not only that, he was told to take her back again later, after she had left him to live with other lovers and return to her old work as a prostitute.

But why?

HIS MESSAGE

Hosea's was a message of God's love, even for His horribly sinful people. Hosea used his own relationship as an example.

The people of Israel were like the unfaithful wife, and God was the loyal husband. The people ran off following other gods, and they were going to be punished for this, but God still loved them and would always take them back if they returned to Him.

BUT WHAT ABOUT ME?

The prophet Hosea shows us God's incredible love. As humans we will never know another love, not even from our parents or our wives or husbands, to compare with the love God has for us. His is a love that we have never deserved, and so we can never do anything that will stop Him loving us. Nothing!

⭐ INTERESTING BITS ||||||||||||||||||||||||||||

The story of Hosea and Gomer – Read Hosea 1:1-9; 3:1-3
God will win back Israel's love – Read Hosea 2:14-23
God has always loved Israel – Hosea 11:1-11

JEREMIAH, LAMENTATIONS, NAHUM, HABAKKUK AND ZEPHANIAH

PROPHETS BEFORE THE FALL OF JUDAH.

THE TIMES THEY LIVED IN

ENEMIES

Talk about high-pressure situations. The people of the southern kingdom must have thought they were caught in some kind of international nutcracker – right between the two greatest empires of the time. Egypt from the south was at war with Babylon in the north – and it looked like Judah was going to be the battleground.

POLITICS

There's no way of staying neutral when war is being fought in your back garden, so the big political question was which side to fight on: Egypt or Babylon? Babylon or Egypt?

In the end, they sided with Egypt – a big mistake which brought the full wrath of the Babylonian empire down on their heads. Before these prophets had stopped speaking, Judah had been destroyed and its people carried into captivity.

LIFESTYLE

As you might imagine, these were nervy times for the people of Judah – no one likes being caught between a rock and a hard place. To make things worse, the Babylonians were even nastier pieces of work than the Assyrians who had led the people of the northern kingdom off with rings through their noses.

There was also a proud belief that nothing bad could happen to Jerusalem, God's holy city. The priests and the king said, 'Don't worry, nothing will happen!' The prophets said, 'Oh yes it will!' The people knew who they wanted to believe, but they weren't quite sure.

RELIGION

You would think that seeing the northern kingdom destroyed as the prophets had predicted would make the people of Judah turn back to God.

Well, for a while this did happen. Under the good king Josiah, there was a mass revival in the southern kingdom. But it didn't last, and soon they were back to their worship of other gods, forgetting the one true God.

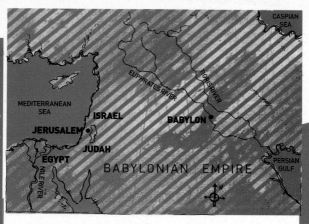

MAP OF THE BABYLONIAN EMPIRE

THE PROPHET
JEREMIAH

A BOOK THAT PREDICTS THE TYPE OF RELATIONSHIP
WITH GOD THAT WE CAN ENJOY TODAY.

THE MAN

There is nothing so despised and low as a traitor. What could be worse than selling out your friends just to save your own skin or to make some money?

Throughout his life, Jeremiah was branded as a traitor and a spy for the Babylonians. Eventually he was arrested, whipped, imprisoned and thrown into a muddy pit to die. He wasn't a traitor, but he did know that the Babylonians were being used by God and it was useless to resist them.

HIS MESSAGE

Jeremiah followed up his message of judgment with a message of hope. It was a hope that one day God would make a new agreement with His people that wouldn't be based upon keeping laws and sacrificing animals, but would involve a personal relationship with God.

BUT WHAT ABOUT ME?

Off goes the alarm, announcing another exhausting day at school. 'I'm just way too tired to bother with reading my Bible or praying – I'll leave that until tomorrow.'

Sometimes keeping in touch with God can seem like hard work, but we need to remember how good we've got it. We have the privilege of living under the new agreement with God that Jeremiah prophesied.

⭐ **INTERESTING BITS** ||||||||||||||||||||||||||||

God calls Jeremiah to be His prophet
– Read Jeremiah 1:1–19
Jeremiah can't stop speaking God's word
– Read Jeremiah 20:7–9
God will make a new agreement
– Read Jeremiah 31:30–34
They treat him like a traitor, but he's proved right in the end – Read Jeremiah 36:1–40:6

THE BOOK OF LAMENTATIONS

Lamentations are sad poems written to describe and mourn the destruction of Jerusalem by the Babylonians. The news-report style shows that they were written by somebody who actually saw all that happened.

THE PROPHET NAHUM

A LESSON ABOUT PRIDE AND HUMILITY.

THE MAN

Nahum was a bit of an undercover operative. We know absolutely nothing about him, except that he was presumably from the nation of Judah. God's mission for him was to prophesy to Nineveh, the capital city of Assyria.

Basically, his message was, 'All right, it's all over for you. God's used you to judge the northern kingdom, but now your time is up and you're going to be destroyed yourselves.' No wonder he needed to operate undercover!

HIS MESSAGE

Sometimes people get a little too big for their boots and have to be taken down a notch or two. Just because God had allowed them to destroy Israel, the Assyrians were under the impression that they were bigger than God. Wrong!

Nahum was assigned by God to prophesy their destruction because it was important that God be proved to be the top dog.

BUT WHAT ABOUT ME?

Have you ever known someone who is really good looking, but totally unattractive because he or she is so sickeningly proud about it? Pride is just so obnoxious.

God feels the same way. He helps humble people, but sooner or later He gives proud people – like the Assyrians – what they deserve. If we know what's good for us, we'll make sure we stay humble.

INTERESTING BITS

Awesome description of God coming to judge
– Read Nahum 1:1–11
When Nineveh falls, everyone will rejoice
– Read Nahum 3:18–19

THE PROPHET
HABAKKUK

AN EXAMPLE FOR US WHEN WE'RE CONFUSED ABOUT LIFE.

THE MAN

Right at the top of my 'to do' list when I get to heaven, before even a quick self-propelled flight around the universe or watching playbacks of creation, is to have a little question and answer session with God. There are some things that I just don't understand.

Habakkuk also had a few tough questions for God.

HIS MESSAGE

Habakkuk was upset at the way things were going. Evil nations like the Babylonians and Assyrians were having a whale of a time, and good people seemed to suffer most. 'Look, God,' he said. 'You've got some explaining to do.'

As he was a prophet, and no doubt far more spiritual than you or I, he got some answers from God – but probably not the ones he would have liked.

God said: 'Be patient, and you'll see.'

BUT WHAT ABOUT ME?

Habakkuk's final response is a perfect example of what God calls all of us to do when we don't understand. Habakkuk declares in a beautiful prayer that no matter how confused he is, no matter how bad things look, he will trust in God anyway.

INTERESTING BITS

The brave prayer of Habakkuk
– Read Habakkuk 3:1–19

THE PROPHET
ZEPHANIAH

A BOOK THAT REMINDS US THAT GOD DOESN'T EXIST JUST TO MAKE US HAPPY.

THE MAN

Another 'wannabe' member of the royal family, Zephaniah
was a distant cousin to King Josiah, in whose reign he
prophesied. Possibly due to Zephaniah's bold prophesying,
as well as that of Jeremiah, there was something of a
national revival and the southern kingdom turned back
towards God.

Sadly, it was too late and too half-hearted – judgment
was still on its way.

HIS MESSAGE

The lottery – imagine the elation, the excitement, the joy,
if your numbers actually came up. But your jaw might drop
and your feelings would do a very abrupt U-turn if it was
then announced that this week's prize was a very long
prison sentence.

That's pretty much the effect that Zephaniah's message
had on the people of Judah. They had a belief that at one
point the 'day of the Lord' would come, and God would
destroy their enemies and elevate them to the position of
greatness they thought they deserved.

'Oh, no!' said Zephaniah. 'The day's coming, but rather
than joy there will be judgment of your sins.'

BUT WHAT ABOUT ME?

God – the sweet old grandfather in the clouds or a heavenly
Father Christmas who gives me whatever I want.

Those attitudes are the modern equivalent of the
expectations of the people of the southern kingdom. Like
them, we sometimes need to be reminded that God doesn't

just exist to give us what we want. He is the Master of the universe, and we need to treat Him with real respect.

INTERESTING BITS

How the 'Day of the Lord' will really be
– Read Zephaniah 1:14–18
Not everyone will be destroyed; some will live to rejoice and serve God again – Read Zephaniah 3:6–20

EZEKIEL AND DANIEL

PROPHETS IN EXILE.

THE TIMES THEY LIVED IN

THE ENEMY

Remember the old joke, 'What do you call a gorilla armed with a machine gun?' The answer is, 'Sir!'

The time for calling the Babylonians 'enemies' had passed – they were definitely in charge. It was now a matter of being as nice to the gorilla as possible, hoping that he wouldn't select you to help him with target practice – by being the target.

POLITICS

Sometimes people just don't get the message.

At first you're kind: 'I'm really sorry, but I'm busy that night.' Then you're clear: 'You're a good friend, but I don't want to go out with you.' Then you have to be brutal: 'You're ugly, my goldfish has more personality and I'd become a nun before I'd go out with you. Get lost!'

The people of the southern kingdom just didn't get the message that the Babylonians had won. The Babylonians first took a small group of hostages, then they took more captives, and finally King Nebuchadnezzar went to war and completely destroyed Jerusalem.

Only when almost the whole nation was taken into captivity did the people realise they'd lost.

LIFESTYLE IN EXILE

If your family has ever had to move because of a parent's change of job, you might have some idea how the people felt about going into exile. They were devastated about leaving their home and everything that they knew, and they were scared of what they might find when they got to the new location.

For most it wasn't too bad. The 'cream' of the southern kingdom society were even allowed to live in the royal palaces. Only the most unlucky were made slaves of the Babylonians.

RELIGION

Painful situations can make us doubt all that we have always believed about God. The exile was a time like that for the people of Judah.

The prophets explained to the people that it wasn't because God was weak that they had been defeated, but because they had walked away from Him. Now that the worst had happened, the prophets began giving hope to the people by prophesying that one day God would take His people back to their land and things would be better than ever before.

THE PROPHET
EZEKIEL

THE MAN

Some people know incredibly early on what career they're going to pursue. They're dressing up in nurses' uniforms or teaching classes composed of dolls and teddy bears, all by the age of five.

Ezekiel was like that. Even as a young man he was very dedicated and trained to become a priest in God's holy Temple in Jerusalem. Unfortunately, his career plans took a serious hit when King Nebuchadnezzar reduced the Temple to a heap of rubble. There were no job opportunities there anymore.

When he was roughly twenty years old, Ezekiel was one of the many people taken away to Babylon as prisoners of war. That was the end of his childhood dreams. But he somehow managed to keep his faith and trust, and five years later God called him to be his prophet to the people living in exile in Babylon.

During this time he saw the most incomprehensible and incredible vision of the holiness and glory of the Lord. It seemed to Ezekiel that he had plugged his fingers into an electricity socket. It was so intense that he fell flat on his face and was in shock for the next seven days.

THE WAY HE SPOKE

I have a gift for forgetting sermons. It doesn't matter how good I think they are while I'm listening, twenty minutes later I can barely remember who was speaking.

Ezekiel was the perfect speaker for people like me, because God often told him to act out his messages to the people. These weren't all funny little skits, though. Some of them were in very bad taste.

At one point, God told Ezekiel to cook his food over a fire of burning human excrement. Ezekiel thought this was going a bit further than was absolutely necessary to make the point, so he persuaded God to let him cook over animal dung instead – oh well, that's fine then!

Other times he had to cut off his hair or lie on one side for hundreds of days. Once he had to act out someone being taken into exile (no problem, he knew all about that experience) to show that soon everyone would be in exile.

HIS MESSAGE

It's amazing how people with a real passion either for something or someone manage to bring it into practically every conversation. 'It's funny that you should mention food, because my gerbil Henry – he's so sweet – has a real partiality to this new pet food I've found. Blah, blah, blah.'

Well, Ezekiel's passion was the Temple. It might be rubble now, but he dreamed of a time when it would be rebuilt and more wonderful than ever before. The people couldn't understand how the Temple could have been destroyed if God was living there.

'Ah,' said Ezekiel. 'It's because He wasn't home.'

That might sound like a stupid explanation to us, but it is exactly what God showed to Ezekiel in a vision. God had been so disgusted with some of the evil things that the people were doing in His holy Temple that He simply left. The people were so far away from God that they didn't even notice He was gone.

God also gave Ezekiel a vision showing that He would return to the Temple.

- -

BUT WHAT ABOUT ME?

Have you ever thought: 'God, where on earth are You? I need You, and You're not here.'

Fortunately, under the new agreement God never actually leaves us, but it is possible for us to walk away from Him for a period of time then suddenly wonder where He is when we need Him.

If we want to avoid the experience of the people of the southern kingdom, who didn't even know God had left until something bad happened, we need to be sure that we keep close to God all the time.

⭐ **INTERESTING BITS** |||||||||||||||||||||||||||||
Ezekiel's call to be a prophet – Read Ezekiel 1:1–3:15
God's presence leaves the Temple – Read Ezekiel 10:1–22
Dead skeletons become alive – Read Ezekiel 37:1–14
God returns to the new Temple – Read Ezekiel 43:1–12

THE PROPHET
DANIEL
A BOOK TO ENCOURAGE CHRISTIANS.

THE MAN

In every school there is sure to be someone who turns you green with envy. They seem too good to be true and make everybody else look stupid, ugly, unathletic and totally ungifted in comparison.

The prophet Daniel must have seemed like that to the people he grew up with. As a young boy from a wealthy family he was taken to Babylon when King Nebuchadnezzar took the first group of hostages. He was chosen along with several others to live in the king's palace and be trained and educated to serve him.

Because of his many talents, Daniel soon became popular and trusted, especially when God added to his already glowing CV or resumé the special gift of being able to interpret dreams.

By the time he had reached old age, Daniel, who had been brought to Babylon as a prisoner of war from an enemy country, had become the right-hand man of the Babylonian king.

HIS MESSAGE
PART 1

The first six chapters of Daniel tell amazing stories about the seventy years that Daniel lived in Babylon. They were written to encourage the people living in captivity in Babylon. They show how God will protect them if they keep their faith in Him.

PART 2

The second part of Daniel is a whole new ball game. If your little brother or sister had dreams like this they'd run crying into your parents' bedroom every night. Even Daniel admits that some of these visions and dreams turned him white with fear.

The dreams are full of weird beasts, monsters and people that talk and crush and destroy. The particular emphasis is on different empires of the world, and on God's kingdom which is greater than them all.

BUT WHAT ABOUT ME?

They may not be Babylon exactly, but our schools, colleges or workplaces can be foreign territory for us as Christians. The stories of Daniel and his friends should encourage us to stand up for God in hostile situations.

⭐ INTERESTING BITS |||||||||||||||||||||||||

Daniel's first experiences in Babylon – Read Daniel 1:1–21
The idol and the fiery furnace – Read Daniel 3:1–30
Daniel's not a dog's/lion's dinner – Read Daniel 6:1–28

HAGGAI, ZECHARIAH AND MALACHI

PROPHETS AFTER THE EXILE.

THE TIME THEY LIVED IN

THE ENEMY

Nothing lasts forever, especially good things like holidays, but also bad things like maths lessons.

The evil Babylonian empire didn't last forever either. In the end, God made sure it was judged for its sins, and it was conquered by the Persians.

The Persians were far more humane rulers, and they allowed the people that the Babylonians had taken into captivity to go home.

POLITICS

Under the Persians, some of the people of Judah were allowed to return home under the leadership of a man called Zerubbabel, grandson of one of the last kings of Judah.

LIFESTYLE

When they talked about it on the way home, around the campfires with the camels snoring in the background, it had seemed so exciting. They couldn't wait to see what God was going to do when they returned to their own land.

But they hadn't counted on how hard things were going to be for them. It is no small thing to rebuild a country from scratch, and often it was difficult to get hold of even the basics, like food and clothes. Also, there was a lot of opposition from the people who had ruled the land since they had left. Naturally, they didn't want to lose their power.

All in all, it wasn't quite the wonderful homecoming the people had imagined for so many years.

RELIGION

The people started off with great enthusiasm for God who had allowed them to return from captivity. They had all the right intentions.

The outward sign of this was how fast they set about trying to rebuild God's Temple, but soon the opposition and the hardship got to them and they began to slack off. They started to think that this 'living in your own country, worshipping your own God' lark wasn't all it was cracked up to be. Their work on the Temple slowed, then came to a complete halt.

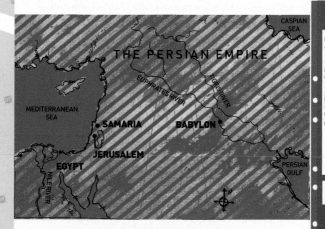

MAP OF THE PERSIAN EMPIRE

THE PROPHET
HAGGAI

A BOOK THAT TEACHES US TO PUT GOD FIRST IN OUR LIVES.

THE MAN

Haggai returned home from exile some time after the first group. As he neared Jerusalem he got more and more excited about the prospect of seeing the great city he had heard so much about, especially the magnificent new Temple that he heard had been built.

When he arrived, all he found was a building site. What's more, he could tell that no work had been done in a very long time. What had gone wrong, he asked?

HIS MESSAGE

Life is all about setting priorities:

'Is it more important that I do my history homework or watch *Match of the Day*? No contest, football is a far higher priority.'

'Should I save this money to give in the offering at church or buy that rather nice pair of jeans? No contest, how I look is much more important than putting a new roof on the church – isn't it?'

The people were busy building their own houses and were no longer concerned about God's house. Haggai told them they had their priorities all wrong. The reason they were struggling was because they weren't putting God first.

BUT WHAT ABOUT ME?

That's a lesson we all need to learn. When we put God first in our lives, whether it's by doing a morning quiet time or putting money into an offering, things will tend to go much better in other areas of our lives.

Encouragement to build the Temple – Read Haggai 1:1–15
A personal prophecy for Zerubbabel
– Read Haggai 2:22–23

⭐ INTERESTING BITS ||||||||||||||||||||||||||

THE PROPHET ZECHARIAH

A BOOK THAT PREDICTS THE LIFE AND DEATH OF JESUS.

THE MAN

'Now look, boys, it's like this. I'm a priest, right? That's how I earn my bread and butter. Well, I can't do any "priesting" until you hurry up and finish building the Temple. So get a move on!'

Zechariah was from a family of priests who returned to Jerusalem. He joined Haggai in encouraging the people to keep working on the Temple.

More importantly, God allowed him to look further into the future to an event even more significant than the rebuilding – the coming of God's Messiah, who we know to be Jesus.

HIS MESSAGE

The first part of Zechariah is a series of visions that all relate to the Temple. In the second section we see many references to Jesus hundreds of years before His birth.

First we rejoice because He will enter Jerusalem riding on a donkey – a sign that His reign will be peaceful, not warlike. Then we see it prophesied that He will be pierced, and people will mourn for Him as if for a lost son or daughter.

Also, we are told that God will provide a fountain that will cleanse people from sin and impurity. We know now that that fountain was Jesus' blood.

THE PROPHET
MALACHI

A BOOK FOR WHEN YOU'RE DISAPPOINTED BY GOD.

THE MAN

Malachi prophesied almost one hundred years after Haggai and Zechariah. Their words had been listened to, and the Temple had been rebuilt, but still the prosperity and wonderful times that the returned people of Judah had expected God to give them had not actually happened. It was always going to be tomorrow, and tomorrow never comes.

The people began to think that God and His prophets had been stringing them along, promising a lot but never delivering the goods. They began to get slack about their worship and their relationship with God. Frankly, they were disappointed.

HIS MESSAGE

God called Malachi to speak to the people, to show them that He hadn't forgotten them.

First Malachi says, 'Remember the good things God has done for you.' For the Israelites this meant comparing themselves with other nations that had been taken by the Babylonians into captivity, but had not been allowed to return home.

Then Malachi said, 'Keep making the effort. Keep treating God right and the good times will come again.'

BUT WHAT ABOUT ME?

It's not unusual to feel let down by God when bad things happen. We have a very different perspective to Him, and we don't understand the way He works in our lives sometimes.

When we feel like that we, like the people of Judah, tend to slacken off in our relationship with and worship of Him. But we need to do the opposite. We should trust Him and spend time with Him so that He can help us through the hard times.

INTERESTING BITS ||||||||||||||||||||||||||

The people aren't wholehearted – Read Malachi 1:6–14
The people rob God – Read Malachi 3:6–18
The final words of the Old Testament – Read Malachi 4:4–6

JOEL, OBADIAH AND JONAH

THE TIMELESS PROPHETS.

At least two of the final three prophets that we will be looking at are very hard to place in terms of their time in history. This doesn't matter, though, as the messages they speak are as relevant to us today as they were when they were written – whenever that was.

THE PROPHET JOEL

THE MAN

You think that your big brother eats a lot. Let me tell you that eating a Big Mac in a single mouthful is nothing compared to the appetite of a swarm of locusts that swept through the southern kingdom. They ate all the crops and destroyed everything in their path. They left the people penniless and in danger of starving.

Joel took the example of this terrible, natural catastrophe and used it as an object lesson to speak about relationship with God.

HIS MESSAGE

Joel told the people that what the locusts had done to them was just a picture of a far more terrible day in the future when God would judge sinful people. God's armies would march through the land like the locusts, only far more powerful and terrifying.

It wasn't all bad news, though. Joel knew that this horror could be averted if the people would repent and turn back to God. If they did this, they would see great things from God.

One of Joel's prophecies was fulfilled in the New Testament when the Holy Spirit was poured out upon the disciples at Pentecost.

⭐ INTERESTING BITS

God's terrible army – Read Joel 2:1–11
The people should repent before God – Read Joel 2:12–17
God promises His Spirit for all people – Read Joel 2:28–32

THE PROPHET
OBADIAH

A BOOK WITH LESSONS ON HOW WE TREAT OTHER PEOPLE.

THE MAN

Obadiah prophesied against a nation called Edom, and it wasn't a nice prophecy at all.

The Edomites were distant relations of the Israelites, but the two nations hated each other and were always fighting. Recently, the Edomites had gloated over Israel's troubles and had actually assisted an enemy nation in attacking Israel – just to make some money.

God sent Obadiah to tell the Edomites that they were going to be judged for that kind of behaviour.

HIS MESSAGE

The Edomites thought that their city was invincible – hidden in the mountains and approached only through a narrow gorge in which enemy soldiers could be killed at will.

'Don't count on it,' said God through Obadiah. 'I'm bigger than that, and you won't escape as easily as you think.'

Sure enough, Edom was totally destroyed by invading Arabs.

BUT WHAT ABOUT ME?

Obadiah's message is sobering for all of us: don't be happy when someone you have a grudge against gets into trouble.

God is concerned even with the way we treat our enemies, and we tend to end up being treated the same way we treat others.

Remember that the next time you're tempted to laugh when your worst enemy gets shown up in class.

Come on, read the whole thing – it's only 21 verses.
Then you can say you've read a complete book of the Bible in one go!

THE PROPHET
JONAH

THE MAN

'Well, sir, I can offer you a berth on the *QE2* next Wednesday, but if you're really desperate there's still some room in the stomach of Moby Dick, the whale, who departs for Nineveh first thing tomorrow morning. We'll supply a peg for your nose as you'll be sharing the space with two tonnes of rotting tuna.'

Everyone has heard of Jonah and his unusual mode of transport, but few of us know what was actually going on in this story.

THE MESSAGE

God had told Jonah to go and preach to the Assyrians in their capital city of Nineveh, to tell them that God was going to judge them for their wickedness. Jonah told God this wasn't a good plan because:

1. They didn't like Israelites, especially not preachy ones.
2. They might escape the judgment if they knew it was coming.

So Jonah ran away, but as we all know it wasn't for long.

BUT WHAT ABOUT ME?

Jonah's message to the Assyrians was 'repent or be judged', but the message of the whole book is about selfishness.

Jonah was concerned only for his own skin and his own country, but God is bigger than that. He is concerned for all the peoples and nations of the world.

Christians also need to remember that God isn't our personal genie who is only there to make things run smoothly for us and our friends. He is concerned about everyone – even our enemies – and our job is to work for Him wherever He calls us.

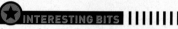
INTERESTING BITS ||||||||||||||||||||||||||||

A treat, it's the fishy bit – Read Jonah 1:14–2:10
God teaches Jonah a lesson – Read Jonah 4:1–11

THE NEW TESTAMENT

FRANCE
AUSTRIA
BULGARIA
BLACK SEA
ITALY
GREECE
SPAIN
TURKEY
SYRIA
MOROCCO
ALGERIA
TUNISIA
MEDITERRANEAN SEA
ISRAEL
LIBYA
EGYPT
JORDAN

SOME MODERN MEDITERRANEAN NATIONS IN THE EARLY 21ST CENTURY

THE ROMAN EMPIRE IN THE EARLY 1ST CENTURY

THE WORLD OF THE NEW TESTAMENT

THE GENTILES (ROMANS AND GREEKS) – EVERYDAY LIFE

2.4 CHILDREN?

What's the biggest risk you've ever taken? Eating your sister's cooking class projects? Or staying in the room when your brother takes off his trainers?

In Roman times, just being born was a huge gamble. A happy or a terrible life depended on the accident of whether you were born a boy or a girl, rich or poor. The rich lived in huge mansions – running water, gardens and heating. But the poorest lived in multi-storey apartment blocks that were a real health hazard – they kept falling down! And you had to learn to keep your legs crossed because they certainly didn't have indoor plumbing.

Girls weren't popular and were often left outside to die as soon as they were born. Some of these unwanted babies were picked up by slave traders and often ended up as prostitutes or priestesses in the temples.

WHAT ABOUT FRIDAY NIGHTS?

It's Friday night. You've got a good-looking date and money in your pocket, but where to go? Without Hollywood to keep them amused, the Greeks and Romans came up with their own entertainments.

The Olympic Games and chariot racing were the big sporting events, but nothing could match the spectacle and excitement of the amphitheatre. Shows in these vast arenas were often gore fests – gladiators fought to the death, ferocious wild animals slaughtered each other, and so much blood was spilt that the soaked sand had to be replaced several times per show!

Other pastimes were equally X-rated: prostitution was common, and pornographic pictures covered the walls of public places. Divorce was easy and frequent, and affairs and violent crimes were common. Sounds a lot like today, doesn't it?

SCHOOLDAZE

Cruelly, girls were prevented from going to school.

'Wait a minute,' I hear you cry. 'What could be cruel about letting me skip school?'

Well, it stopped girls from becoming educated and living as full a life as boys. Boys would start by being taught by a family slave, then go on to one of the major universities in places like Athens or Rhodes.

AT WORK

If you visited a careers officer in those times, he might recommend many jobs still popular today. There were bankers, shop assistants, farmers, sailors, soldiers – even dentists and doctors.

THE RELIGIOUS WORLD OF THE GENTILES
MYTHOLOGY

The Greeks had invented a complicated family of gods and goddesses whom they worshipped.

The top job went to Zeus, who ruled from Mount Olympus. His subjects were immortal and incredibly powerful, but otherwise behaved like naughty schoolchildren – always stealing, arguing and fighting.

There were many temples to these gods in ancient cities. Priests, priestesses and prophets tried to guide the people in their attempts to communicate with the gods.

THE ROMAN RELIGIONS

The Romans took the Greek gods and gave them Roman names. Few people really trusted or wholly believed in these unlikable gods, but they kept up the pretence of worshipping them, perhaps because they were scared. If the gods were known for anything it was for their cruelty to humans who displeased them.

Dead Roman emperors were also thought of as gods, and certain living emperors began to demand that people worship and pray to them as well. This caused the Christians lots of problems as their refusal to worship the emperor was considered rebellion.

MYSTERY RELIGIONS

Remember Enid Blyton's *Secret Seven* stories? Not many adults find those kids' books thrilling, but some people never grow out of secret clubs with special signs, languages and meeting places.

Secret religious 'clubs' were very popular in Roman times. Because they were so, so secret we really don't know much about what they stood for. What we do know is that they had special signs and handshakes for recognising one another, and that you had to swear bloodthirsty oaths of secrecy to become a member. Some of what they got up to in their meetings can't be mentioned on the same page as a nice children's writer like Enid Blyton.

SUPERSTITION

Greeks and Romans had some weird ways of predicting the future.

They followed the stars and horoscopes, but they also watched the flight of birds, poured oil onto water and watched the way it moved, and split open dead animals to see in what order their guts fell out. Yuck!

They also believed in magic and demons, and people made lots of money by selling spells or special charms, and by doing weird dances or ceremonies to chase off evil spirits.

GENERAL

Few of the millions of people in the Roman Empire followed either a particular religion or a particular philosophy. Most were simply superstitious. Religiously, they lived in a frightening fog where hideous shapes appeared and disappeared, cruel gods played wicked games with their lives, and nobody seemed to be able to make sense of it for them.

This meant that many were open to Christianity when it came, because it offered a loving and caring God and answers to the questions of the universe.

THE JEWS – EVERYDAY LIFE
NOT QUITE 2.4 CHILDREN

Jewish families tended to be large and much closer (literally) than the Romans and Greeks. You could forget about getting your own bedroom – the average family, and their animals, all slept in one room. (At least there were plenty of other suspects if the baked beans you ate for dinner had their usual effect.)

Sadly, sexism existed in Jewish families too. The birth of a baby boy caused great rejoicing, while the birth of a girl was considered a disappointment. If a Jewish family member died, they were certainly made to feel missed. The whole family wailed and tore their clothes, and perhaps even paid professional mourners to come in and do the job properly.

LOVE AND MARRIAGE

Frightening thought – what if your parents picked the person you were to marry? ('But, Dad, she has to shave more often than I do!') That is exactly what happened to young Jewish men and women.

It does seem that the would-be bride and groom had some opportunity to protest, but this would probably be severely frowned upon by the rest of the family. So you had to hope your mum and dad had good taste!

Boyfriend and girlfriend relationships were unheard of. Many girls would have been married or at least betrothed (a strict engagement) by the time they were teenagers, so there wasn't much time for tongue-tangles behind the bike sheds.

This explains the Bible's lack of advice (the difference between a holy and an unholy kiss would be useful) for this sort of relationship.

SCHOOLDAZE
Young Jewish children were given a very basic education by their parents – in Jewish history and religion, and in practical skills such as potty training and beyond.

At the age of about six the boys would go on to the synagogue schools. Here the Old Testament was the text book: for maths ('Count the words in the book of Joshua'); for history (that's Old Testament history); for biology ('Now, when King David saw Bathsheba in the bath ...').

All Jewish boys were also taught a trade. Remember, Jesus was trained as a carpenter.

If you wanted more schooling (it happens, you know), you found an older rabbi or teacher and became his personal pupil.

What about the girls? Well, they stayed at home learning more practical skills – potty training their younger brothers and sisters perhaps?

AT WORK
Most Jewish men followed the trade that they had been trained in as boys. Fishermen, farmers, shopkeepers and carpenters were common.

If you liked being loathed and spat at every time you walked out of your door, you could always become a tax collector. The Jews hated the fact that the Romans, accursed Gentiles, were in control of their country. And they hated any of their fellow countrymen who helped the Romans or made money out of their being there – like tax collectors. This is why people were so shocked when Jesus ate, or even spoke, with tax collectors.

JEWISH RELIGIOUS LIFE

Every school has the sort of wimp who's all macho mouth when ten of his friends are around, but will cower before a junior school weakling when he's on his own. That was the way with the Greek gods, such a sorry bunch that there had to be loads of them.

The Jews needed only one God – the Almighty YAHWEH. His history with them as His chosen people was recorded in their sacred book – what we call the Old Testament.

MISTAKEN IDENTITY

Have you ever built up a picture in your mind of what someone must be like – then you meet them and they're totally different?

The Jews were waiting for a Messiah sent by God, but when Jesus turned up most didn't recognise Him. They were looking for someone completely different – a brilliant general who would throw out the Romans, or a brilliant ruler to reign on earth forever. They didn't expect God Himself in human form, they didn't expect Him to be born to a virgin, and they didn't expect Him to die and rise again.

THE SYNAGOGUE

Big, thick Swiss Army knives are the business. I bet that in a few years' time there will be a blade that pops up and becomes a mobile phone, and one that tells you the answers to your maths homework.

The synagogue was the Swiss Army knife of the Jewish life, and the centre of each Jewish community. A school was only one of its many functions.

The simple rectangular room, with a raised platform at one end and a big chest which contained the valuable Old Testament scrolls, was: a church on Sabbath days; the place for political meetings; a court for Jewish law; a funeral home; and a help centre for the poor.

THE TEMPLE

While there were many synagogues, there was only one Temple – a huge and magnificent building in the city of Jerusalem.

The outer parts of the Temple could be entered by Gentile tourists, but there were huge signs in different languages forbidding anyone but Jews to enter the inner courts – on pain of death. It was in the Temple that the animal sacrifices were made by the priests.

A WHO'S WHO OF JEWISH GROUPS

This is a quick guide to some of the Jewish religious groups you might meet as you read the New Testament.

Pharisees – These guys get a raw deal when we read the New Testament. They tried their best to keep the Old Testament Law, but took things a little too far: 'Don't spit on the ground on the Sabbath because the dirt might move, and that's practically ploughing which is forbidden.' They had also become proud of themselves and looked down on other people. That really got Jesus' goat.

Sadducees – Many of the priests who worked in the Temple were Sadducees. They were growing rich by working closely with the Romans, and they didn't believe in life after death, angels, demons or anything as primitive as that.

Scribes – This term really describes the profession of these men. They were part lawyer, part teacher, part professional secretary. They taught and interpreted the Law that God had given to the Jews in the Old Testament.

Sanhedrin – It was in front of the Sanhedrin that Jesus was tried before His crucifixion. It was the highest court of the Jews and was made up of members of all the groups named above.

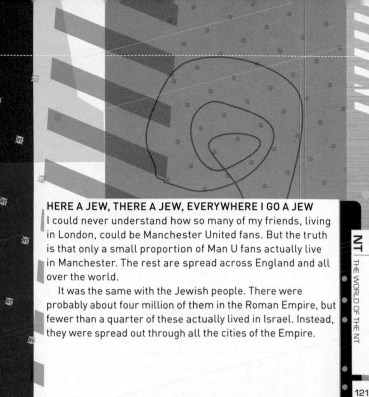

HERE A JEW, THERE A JEW, EVERYWHERE I GO A JEW

I could never understand how so many of my friends, living in London, could be Manchester United fans. But the truth is that only a small proportion of Man U fans actually live in Manchester. The rest are spread across England and all over the world.

It was the same with the Jewish people. There were probably about four million of them in the Roman Empire, but fewer than a quarter of these actually lived in Israel. Instead, they were spread out through all the cities of the Empire.

THE **FOUR** GOSPELS

GENERAL INTRODUCTION

Two thousand years ago the world was rocked to its very core. Not by a meteor or something else from outer space, but by a Man – Jesus of Nazareth. He split world history in two. Before His birth, BC – after, AD. We can meet Him in the four Gospels.

DEFINITION OF 'GOSPEL'

Imagine living in an ancient city at war. Every morning you wake up in fear of invading enemy soldiers stealing, raping and murdering. If a messenger arrived saying your side had won and you were free, it would be good news wouldn't it?

Well, that kind of good news is what the word 'gospel' originally meant. In time it was attached to the four books which had been written about Jesus' life – because they told the good news of the battle He had won for us.

WHY WERE THEY WRITTEN?

The apostles, who had known and lived with Jesus, became increasingly important – like human 'hard-drives' full of information about Him. But, darn them, they began to grow old – and die.

The race was on to record all that they knew about Jesus'
life before it was too late. God inspired some of them – and
other authors working with them – to write the Gospels.

BUT WHY ARE THERE FOUR?

All sorts of designers, from civil engineers to artistic
fashion students, use nifty computer software for their
work. The big advantage of software like this is that it is
possible to work not just in two dimensions, like on paper,
but in three – like the real world. A 3D image on a computer
can be turned around and viewed from every side.

If God had inspired only one author to write one account of
Jesus, it would have been very useful, but one dimensional.
Since we have four, all looking at Jesus from a slightly
different angle, it is like seeing Him in three – or even four –
dimensions.

HOW ARE THEY RELATED?

If Matthew, Mark and Luke had placed their three 'essays'
in front of an English examiner, there would have been big
trouble and some accusations of cheating flying around.

It is generally believed that Mark was written first, and
that Matthew and Luke used his Gospel as the basis for
the flow of action in their accounts. In some places they
blatantly copied.

This was common and acceptable practice in ancient
times. It doesn't discount their historical accuracy, or make
God's inspiration and involvement any less.

A LIFE OF JESUS

If you tried to write a sort of music fanzine article about
Jesus, it would be pretty boring. There are no photos
available, for a start.

Today, we like to know absolutely everything about
famous people – from the colour of their boxer shorts, to
their favourite brand of deodorant, and with whom they
enjoyed their first kiss.

It wasn't the same when Jesus was around. Although His life is better documented than any other ancient person, we still don't know much about the personal details. If we put together everything we know, a chart would look like this.

EVENTS OF JESUS' LIFE

1   Announcement of birth

2   Birth

3   Presentation in the Temple

4   While still an infant, secretly hurried into Egypt by His parents

5   Baptised by His relative, probably cousin, John

6   Selected the Twelve (His first disciples)

7   Rejected by His hometown (Nazareth)

8   Preached the Sermon on the Mount (possibly the greatest message ever)

9   Calmed a storm with just His words

10 Fed more than 5,000 people (on at least two occasions)

11 Right in front of three close friends, He was transfigured (for just a moment, He put on as much of His God-ness as His friends could stand without being incinerated on the spot)

12 Gave life back to Lazarus (who was dead, buried and beginning to stink by the time Jesus arrived on the scene)

13 Blessed children

14 Was crucified, buried and resurrected

15 Ascended into heaven

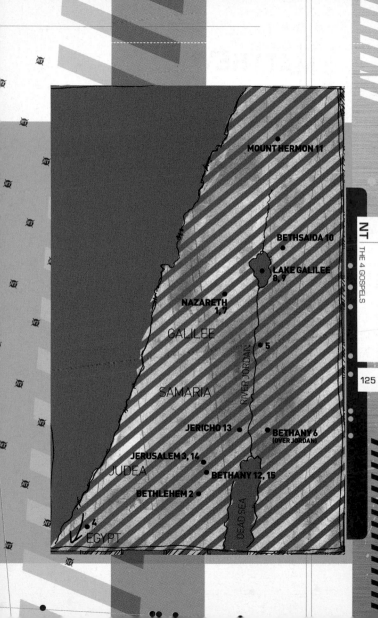

MOUNT HERMON 11

BETHSAIDA 10

LAKE GALILEE
8, 9

NAZARETH
1, 7

GALILEE

5

RIVER JORDAN

SAMARIA

JERICHO 13

BETHANY 6
(OVER JORDAN)

JERUSALEM 3, 14

JUDEA

BETHANY 12, 15

BETHLEHEM 2

EGYPT

DEAD SEA

THE GOSPEL OF
MATTHEW

SO WHAT'S MATTHEW'S ANGLE?

Some people's feet smell bad enough when you're standing up and are 5 or 6 feet away, but being down there at ground level trying to squeeze into a the hot, sweaty and swollen foot of some Saturday afternoon shopper shoe must be hellish. Pity the shoe shop workers!

Matthew's Gospel is like the shoehorn that helps fit the New Testament (the foot) into the already formed back-ground (the shoe) of the Old Testament. In Matthew, we see Jesus as the Jewish Messiah – the fulfilment of God's Old Testament promises to the Jewish people. Matthew makes the perfect link between the Old and the New Testaments.

BUT WHO WAS MATTHEW?

Matthew was the Jewish tax collector who became a disciple of Jesus.

Note the fact that only Matthew reports the strange story about Jesus, Peter, a fish and the Temple tax (read the whole thing in Matthew 17:24–27).

WHEN DID HE WRITE IT?

As Matthew used Mark's Gospel as the basis of his, then obviously his must have been written later. Duh!

Since it seems to be written primarily for Jews, it was probably written in the middle of the first century when the majority of the Christians were Jewish. It might have been written around AD 50.

WHO WAS HE WRITING TO?

Matthew wrote especially for Jewish Christians who were being persecuted. He encourages them to use even persecution as an opportunity for evangelism.

Matthew would also expect his book to be read by other people.

OLD TESTAMENT PROPHECY

Many times I've wished I had a prophetic gifting – it would cut down hugely on revision time if I could predict what questions were going to come up in an exam. It seems, though, that God only speaks to His prophets about important things – exams probably don't count.

Event after event in Jesus' life is shown by Matthew to have been predicted by Old Testament prophets:

The virgin birth – Read Matthew 1:22–23
The birthplace, Bethlehem – Read Matthew 2:5–6
The entry to Jerusalem on a donkey – Read Matthew 21:4–5

In the past, people have argued that the Early Christians simply invented parts of Jesus' life in order to make it conform to Old Testament prophecy. But this is not borne out by the facts.

The story of Jesus' life came first, and it was only later that the disciples noticed that certain events had been predicted in the Old Testament.

JESUS' COMPASSION

Jesus is sometimes described, especially in old versions of the Bible, as 'meek'. You might think that's a horrible way to be described. Some people may picture a mummy's boy or a girl's blouse (excuse the sexism). What does it mean?

I'll never forget a scene I saw on TV in the middle of a rugby international. A big and exceptionally ugly second row forward, who shall remain nameless for that reason, was kneeling on the field with a badly injured player's head on his lap. He was holding his hand and stroking his forehead to comfort him. That's meekness – the strength of a second row forward expressed in kindness and gentleness.

That's how we see Jesus in Matthew's Gospel. Of course, He's the Messiah, the powerful Son of God, but He is often moved by compassion for the people He sees around Him.

JESUS' MANIFESTO

Opinions are like armpits. Everyone has a couple, and most of them stink. It's not unusual for people to give their opinion of how life should be lived. It is unique to find one as different, radical and beautiful as Jesus' view.

Discover all about how Jesus thought people should live and treat one another by reading the most famous sermon ever given.

BUT WHAT ABOUT ME?

Jesus truly was a revolutionary. He was incredibly powerful but chose to use His power to show kindness to people who needed it. Read Matthew and be challenged to follow Jesus' revolutionary way of living.

INTERESTING BITS

The Sermon on the Mount (see above)
– Read Matthew 5:1–7:29
The parable of the sheep and the goats
– Read Matthew 25:32–46
Incredible signs accompany Jesus' death
– Read Matthew 27:45–56

THE GOSPEL OF
MARK

WHAT WAS MARK'S ANGLE?

Convincing your parents of the suitability of your latest boyfriend or girlfriend can be difficult. ('But, Mum, everyone's forehead is tattooed now, and body piercing is cool. Oh! You are so old-fashioned!') But trying to convince them of the eligibility of someone condemned to die in the electric chair would be even harder.

This is something like the problem the Early Christians faced. Whatever else they told people about Jesus, they often came unstuck when they said He had been crucified. For people of that time, that was the most shameful and unpleasant end imaginable.

Mark tried to counteract the shame of Jesus' death on the cross by showing how incredible His life was.

WHO WROTE IT?

Very early tradition says John Mark, a man who travelled with Paul and was the cousin of Barnabas. He also acted as the apostle Peter's interpreter.

Mark is reported to have recorded lots of short stories and anecdotes that Peter told here and there, and formed them into one continuous account of Jesus' life.

WHEN WAS IT WRITTEN?

Mark's Gospel was probably written in the late forties of the first century AD, when Peter was in Rome.

WHO WAS IT WRITTEN FOR?

Mark's careful explanations of Jewish customs and tradition implies that it was written for Gentiles, especially Romans who would have found Jesus' death on a cross most off-putting.

MAIN THEME

A GOSPEL OF ACTION

Mark's Jesus is like Action Man – constantly on an important mission. Places to go, people to see, enemies to fight.

If you wanted to tell a non-Christian friend where to start reading the Bible, then Mark's – the shortest and most action-packed Gospel – would be best.

BUT WHAT ABOUT ME?

Need the basic facts on what Jesus said and did? Mark is the place to look.

INTERESTING BITS

Predicting the future – Read Mark 13:1–37
In this chapter, Jesus predicts two future events: the destruction of the Temple in Jerusalem; and the end of the world when He will return in all His glory.

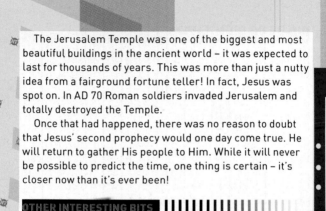

The Jerusalem Temple was one of the biggest and most beautiful buildings in the ancient world – it was expected to last for thousands of years. This was more than just a nutty idea from a fairground fortune teller! In fact, Jesus was spot on. In AD 70 Roman soldiers invaded Jerusalem and totally destroyed the Temple.

Once that had happened, there was no reason to doubt that Jesus' second prophecy would one day come true. He will return to gather His people to Him. While it will never be possible to predict the time, one thing is certain – it's closer now than it's ever been!

OTHER INTERESTING BITS ||||||||||||||||||||||||

Jesus' power over the most violent demons
– Read Mark 5:1–20
John the Baptist's head on a plate – Read Mark 6:14–29
Cost and reward of following Jesus – Read Mark 10:17–31
There's surfing and then there's surfing
– Read Mark 4:35–41 and Mark 6:45–50

DID HE OR DIDN'T HE?

Do you want to know a really good way to become a Christian? A really cool way is to start to try to prove that Jesus didn't really rise from the dead.

A number of very clever lawyers have tried to prove once and for all that it didn't happen. They wanted to help people not to be confused by all those stupid Christian stories – wasn't that sweet of them? But instead, each of them has become a Christian and now believes in the literal physical resurrection of Jesus' body from the dead. They even argue that if the case was tried in a court of law, the resurrection would prove to be the only reasonable explanation of what happened.

There's no space here to examine all the evidence, but just consider these problems with the main theories of those who say Jesus didn't rise from the dead.

THEORY 1
Some say Jesus didn't actually die. But:
1. The Roman soldiers who knew their job said He did.
2. The blood and watery liquid that came out of the stab wound in His side proves He did.
3. That's not to mention a brutal beating, six hours on a cross, and the fact that He was embalmed, wrapped up like a mummy and placed in a tomb.

THEORY 2

Some say the disciples stole the corpse. But:

1. They were far too scared to even consider it.
2. There were Roman soldiers guarding the tomb who were liable to be executed if they let the 'prisoner' escape.
3. The tomb was found in perfect order, with even the burial clothes neatly folded – scarcely the work of frantic grave robbers.

THEORY 3

Still others say the disciples were hallucinating, or simply made the whole thing up. But:

1. Five hundred people don't hallucinate the same thing, and in 1 Corinthians 15 Paul practically begs doubters to go and ask one of the many eyewitnesses.
2. If it was all made up, why didn't the non-believers simply go and get the rotting, smelly corpse and throw it down in front of the overly imaginative disciples? That would have been embarrassing for them, and probably the end of their made-up resurrection stories.
3. Finally, in spite of the fact that almost all of the disciples were martyred for their belief in Jesus, not one of them ever even gave a hint that it might be a hoax. Not many con-men would be so committed as to die for their scam.

Even if you don't believe that the Bible is the inspired Word of God, you'll really have a problem trying to find a better explanation than the one put forward by Matthew, Mark, Luke and John.

THE GOSPEL OF
LUKE

WHAT'S LUKE'S ANGLE?

'Know-it-alls' really drive me mad. Name any subject under the sun and they have facts, figures and quotes to relate to you at great length. You're chatting happily with your best mate about Brad Pitt's latest film, and along comes 'Mr or Miss Know-it-all' with information on everything from which dentist polishes his sparkling white teeth, to how many times a year Brad and Angelina visit the mother-in-law. Do we really care?

Luke is the know-it-all of the New Testament. He tells us that he did lots of careful research before he wrote this orderly account to prove the truth of Christianity. Where did Jesus get His beard trimmed? Luke would have known.

WHO WROTE IT?

The Gospel of Luke definitely fits with the book of Acts and was written by the same author. For more information on him look ahead to Acts.

It is quite likely that Luke wrote his Gospel while staying in Rome with the apostle Paul, who was imprisoned there.

WHEN WAS IT WRITTEN?

Luke's Gospel was written in Rome in the early sixties of the first century AD.

WHO WAS IT WRITTEN TO?

Have you ever heard of Theophilus? (I bet he loved his mum and dad for giving him that name.) That's who Luke dedicates his book to. Theophilus might have been a recent convert, a potential convert, perhaps the person who provided the money for Luke to write his books.

Luke wrote mostly for open-minded Gentiles who were genuinely interested in the historical origins of Christianity even if they were not yet Christians themselves.

MAIN THEMES ||||||||||||||||||||||||||||||||||

JESUS – THE MAN OF PRAYER

Luke shows that Jesus was a man of prayer, praying either at or before all the important events of His life and ministry.

Jesus was praying at His baptism – Read Luke 3:21
Jesus prayed all night before He chose the twelve apostles – Read Luke 6:12
Jesus was praying as He was transfigured
– Read Luke 9:28
Jesus prayed before His arrest and crucifixion
– Read Luke 22:41

The disciples didn't fail to notice the effectiveness of Jesus' prayers and decided that they'd like a little bit of that power too – if you please. What Jesus taught them must have blown them away.

'Abba' Father. We can have no idea how radical it would have been for the Jewish disciples to be told to address their God as 'My "Daddy" Father'. That phrase showed how totally different faith was going to be now that Jesus had come.

ONE FOR ALL AND ALL FOR ONE

If you're a bit of a social campaigner, if you like to spend your Christmases feeding the homeless, or if you like working for charities, then Luke is the Gospel for you.

Luke shows that Jesus was the special friend of the hurting people in society. People who are rejected and hurt by others are particular objects of God's love given through Jesus. The sick people, the poor people, the despised people like tax collectors and prostitutes, loved to be with Jesus because He treated them so well and wasn't embarrassed to be seen with them.

Women, who were considered of only slightly more value than animals in Jesus' day(!), also found a champion in Jesus. He respected them as much as any man, allowed them to listen to and be taught by Him along with His closest disciples, and even appeared first to them after His resurrection.

LUKE

BUT WHAT ABOUT ME?

Jesus cares passionately about outsiders. Great news for us if we feel we're being left out and overlooked. Also great news for any outsiders we know. Let's not forget to share this news with them.

INTERESTING BITS

For info on Jesus as baby and child – Read Luke 1:1–2:52
The story of the good Samaritan – Read Luke 10:25–37
The story of the lost son – Read Luke 15:11–32
Increasingly incredible miracles – Read Luke 8:40–56
Jesus sends out seventy-two missionaries
– Read Luke 10:1–24
A section about feasts and banquets – Read Luke 14:1–24

THE GOSPEL OF
JOHN

WHAT WAS JOHN'S ANGLE?

When you first start going out with someone, it's all wonderful. You both act just the way you think the other person wants you to, and for a while it all seems too good to be true. Sooner or later, though, you have to start getting to know the real person inside – and often that's when the trouble starts.

John wanted to take his readers to a new level of relationship with Jesus. He wanted them to know the Person inside. With Jesus, though, the deeper you go the more wonderful it gets.

WHO WROTE IT?

The best biographies – the ones that really dish the dirt – come from 'insiders', people close to the central character. This Gospel is full of the sort of details only an eyewitness would remember, and the author calls himself the 'disciple whom Jesus loved'. This is not pride – nowhere does he call himself by name – but it fits with what we know of the disciple John from the other Gospels.

This Gospel is very precious as it was written by someone who knew Jesus so intimately.

WHEN WAS IT WRITTEN?

Nobody is sure exactly when it was written, but it is possible that John wrote it anywhere between AD 60 and AD 90.

MAIN THEMES ||||||||||||||||||||||||||||||||||||||

JESUS THE GOD–MAN

Is it a bird? Is it a plane? No, it's the God–man.

John's Gospel helps us to understand that Jesus was both really God and really a man. He wasn't a man pretending to be God, nor God just pretending to be a man, but both. Try wrapping your brain around that one!

At the beginning of his Gospel, John makes the outrageous claim that Jesus, called the Word of God, was actually the creative force behind the formation of the universe (1:3). Then He became 'clothed' in human flesh so that He could come down to earth to stay a little while with us (1:14). All this so that He could reveal the God who had never before been seen to all of us on earth (1:18).

Jesus didn't stop being God when He came to earth. John shows this especially in what are called Jesus' 'I AM' claims.

I AM the bread of life– Read John 6:35
I AM the light of the world – Read John 8:12
I AM the resurrection and the life – Read John 11:25
I AM the way and the truth and the life – Read John 14:6

These claims are bold. No normal man could make them unless he was: (a) high on something stronger than aspirin; or (b) a sandwich short of a picnic.

But the claims didn't annoy the Jews so much as the times when Jesus simply said, 'I AM' (full stop). 'I AM' was how God revealed Himself to Moses in the Old Testament, so in these instances Jesus was making clear claims to be God. This is why in chapter 8, verses 58–59, they immediately pick up stones to kill Him. Stoning was the punishment for blasphemy and, of course, calling yourself God was obviously blasphemy – unless like Jesus you really were God!

John had to balance this emphasis on Jesus as God with proof that He was also really a man. He does this by showing that Jesus got tired and thirsty (4:6–7 and 19:28), that He wept (11:35), and that He really died and rose again (19:30–42 and 20:12–28).

BUT WHAT ABOUT ME?

Jesus is God – no doubt about it! So let's worship Him. But He also knows exactly what it's like to be human. So whatever we're going through, Jesus understands.

INTERESTING BITS ||||||||||||||||||||||||||||

The story behind the famous John 3:16 verse
– Read John 3:1–21
An evening with Jesus – Read John 13–17
Jesus and the Samaritan woman – Read John 4:1–42
Jesus protects the adulterous woman – Read John 8:1–11
Jesus after the resurrection – Read John 20–21

THE FOUR GOSPELS

ACTS

NT

ROMANS
1 CORINTHIANS
2 CORINTHIANS
GALATIANS
EPHESIANS
PHILIPPIANS
COLOSSIANS
1 THESSALONIANS
2 THESSALONIANS
1 TIMOTHY
2 TIMOTHY
TITUS
PHILEMON

PAUL'S LETTERS

HEBREWS
JAMES
1 PETER
2 PETER
1 JOHN
2 JOHN
3 JOHN
JUDE

OTHER LETTERS

REVELATION

REVELATION

THE **ACTS** OF THE **APOSTLES**

INTRODUCTION

Acts tells the story of an explosion – the dynamic beginnings of the Christian Church. The fuse is lit when Jesus returns to heaven, and the flames ignite when the Holy Spirit is poured out on the disciples. There are fireworks and spectacular results as they proclaim the good news about Jesus.

In a series of secondary explosions, the gospel is carried from Jerusalem to the city that was then the centre of the world – Rome.

WHO WROTE IT?

You can tell a doctor from a mile off. Even if there's no obvious visual sign – like one of those wooden tongue depressor thingies stuck behind the ear – you can tell because they insist on calling everything by its proper medical name.

Greek scholars have noticed that the author of Acts was the sort of man who insisted on calling bad breath 'halitosis'. He could only have been a doctor.

Luke, who wrote a Gospel as well as Acts, was possibly Paul's personal doctor. He certainly travelled with him a lot. One of the first Gentiles to become a Christian, he probably lived in the city of Antioch. He knew how to look after himself, because he was reputed to have lived to eighty-four years of age – a great innings for those times.

TYPE OF WRITING

Sneaking a peek into someone's personal organiser can be fun – finding out what they've got scheduled for Saturday nights, for instance. But if you get hold of their diary, then you've hit pay dirt – not just dates and appointments, but thoughts and feelings too.

The book of Acts is more like a diary than an organiser. It records past events – so it is history – but it's more than simple facts. Luke's intention was to show God working in the history he wrote, and to encourage people who read his book in their belief and understanding of God.

HISTORICALLY TRUE?

Fortunately for us, Luke is a real Sherlock Holmes. He has a sharp eye for small and seemingly unimportant details, and is meticulously accurate. Like any great detective he made notes on things he saw himself, interviewed witnesses and consulted other accounts of what had happened. So, we can trust that what we read about in Acts really took place.

WHEN AND WHERE WAS THIS BOOK WRITTEN?

Have you ever watched one of those old Saturday morning serials – *Flash Gordon* or *Batman* maybe? Remember the way they leave you hanging? Batman about to be chopped in two by a falling axe. Flash about to crash his rocket into a meteor.

Acts leaves one of its main heroes in just such a sticky predicament. Why would Luke finish his book with Paul stuck in prison and all us readers wondering whether he was going to be executed or not?

The most reasonable explanation is that this is how things stood at the time that Luke wrote the book. Luke might even have written a lot of the book sitting in that prison cell in Rome with the apostle Paul! Maybe around AD 63.

SO WHY DID HE WRITE IT?

After returning from a holiday in Greece, you might need
to write two letters: one to your great-aunt Maude, and one
to your best friend. Just by reading them it would be easy
to tell which was which. For instance, your aunt probably
wouldn't need to know about the person you kissed/didn't
quite kiss/wished you hadn't kissed.

By studying Luke's books, we can guess who he was
writing to and why he was writing. Luke probably didn't
write Acts for Christians. Instead, he wrote for two groups
of non-Christians.

The first group were people who were genuinely
interested in Christianity but were not yet convinced. They
needed solid proof that it was not just made-up stories.

Secondly, Luke was writing for the Roman rulers. He
wanted them to understand Christianity and trust that its
followers were not dangerous rebels.

OUTLINE OF THE BOOK OF ACTS

1:1–2:47	The birth of the Christian Church
3:1–5:42	Church leaders confront Jewish leaders
6:1–9:31	The Church grows and spreads
9:32–12:25	Non-Jews join the Church
13:1–14:28	Paul's first missionary journey
15:1–35	Church leaders discuss non-Jewish Christians
15:36–20:38	Paul's second and third missionary journeys
21:1–28:31	Paul's arrest, trials and journey to Rome

MAIN THEMES ||||||||||||||||||||||||||||||||

THE HOLY SPIRIT

Wonder Woman spun around, Superman disappeared into telephone booths to put on his red underpants, Batman had the Batcave for his transformation – but what happened to Peter?

In the Gospels, Peter is keen but often incompetent and cowardly. In Acts he is transformed. He is fearless, he is able to perform powerful miracles (even his shadow could heal), he has overcome his previous 'foot in mouth disease' and become a powerful speaker. What had happened to this man?

Luke's answer is that he had been filled with the Spirit. One of the main emphases of Acts is that the Holy Spirit empowers people to live the Christian life, and particularly to be witnesses of Jesus.

GOOD NEWS – FOR EVERYONE!

Some things just don't mix. Oil and water, Friday nights and homework, cricket balls and greenhouses. Add to that list Jews and the rest of the world.

The Jewish disciples suffered a severe case of 'selective hearing' (you know what I mean – the condition that allows you to hear your mum calling, 'Do you need some money?', but totally miss 'Clean up your room') when Jesus told them to take the good news to everyone. They assumed that He meant every Jew.

Around the middle of Acts, though, a totally unexpected thing happens – non-Jews start becoming Christians! In fact, within a short time they vastly outnumber the Jewish believers.

THE APOSTLE PAUL

It's important to match people's abilities to the role that you want them to perform. It's no use having someone who's tone deaf as the singer in a band, and someone of five feet nothing is unlikely to make it as a top class goalkeeper.

The apostle Paul's background and abilities made him the

perfect man for the job God wanted him to perform. He was a devout and academically brilliant Jew, but he was also a Roman citizen who had grown up in the Gentile city of Tarsus.

To begin with, he passionately hated the Christians, but he was miraculously converted and went on to become a very important man in the New Testament. His unusual background helped him to relate to and be a link between the Jews and the Gentiles. His past studies helped him to explain the Christian message better than anyone else. Eventually he was arrested and sent to Rome where he was probably martyred for his faith in Jesus.

 BUT WHAT ABOUT ME?

Incredible stuff! Acts shows just how much God can do through ordinary people like us, if we let Him have His way. Inspiring or what?!

INTERESTING BITS ||||||||||||||||||||||||||||

READ ABOUT PAUL'S MISSIONARY JOURNEYS:
Journey One – Acts 13:1–14:28
– 1,500 miles – Testing the water
Journey Two – Acts 15:36–18:22
– 4,000 miles – First into Europe
Journey Three – Acts 18:23–21:19
– 4,000 miles – Ends in Jerusalem

In Paul's life, and particularly in his missionary journeys, we see how God can use people who are willing to take outrageous risks for Him.

OTHER INTERESTING BITS ||||||||||||||||||||||||||

The Holy Spirit at Pentecost – Read Acts 2:1–41
Don't mess with God – Read Acts 5:1–11
The conversion of Saul/Paul – Read Acts 9:1–13
Tales of the high seas – Read Acts 27:1–28:10
Ever fallen asleep during a sermon? – Read Acts 20:7–12

PAUL'S LETTERS

GENERAL INTRODUCTION

THE LETTER WRITER

Serious workaholic, insomniac or what? Paul, the Christian-hater transformed into Christian leader, not only travelled all over the known world as a missionary, but also found time to write thirteen of the books of the New Testament.

BOOKS OR LETTERS?

Reading other people's post may be rude, but that's just what you're doing in a lot of the New Testament. Each of Paul's New Testament books takes the form of a letter. Some are written to whole churches or regions, and some to individuals.

In our Bibles, letters to whole churches come first, and those to individuals second. Each group is arranged from the longest to the shortest.

HEY, THIS IS DEEP – WHAT DOES IT MEAN?

Any snoop who's ever tried to read someone else's letters knows it's a bit like listening to one side of a telephone conversation. You can hear the answers but have to guess at the questions – you'd catch so much more if you just knew what the other person was saying.

This is why we need to know something about the people and places Paul was writing to. It's like hearing at least some of the other side of the conversation and makes reading Paul's letters much more interesting and informative.

WHERE DID HE FIND THE TIME?

The time to write letters might have fitted into Paul's very crowded life like this:

Paul's birth	around the same time as Jesus
Paul's conversion	AD 33
First missionary journey	AD 47–48
Galatians written after return	AD 48
Council at Jerusalem	AD 49
Second missionary journey	AD 49–52
1 and 2 Thessalonians written (during)	AD 52
Third missionary journey	AD 52–56
1 and 2 Corinthians written (during)	AD 55
Romans written (during)	AD 56
Arrest in Jerusalem	AD 56
Journey to Rome	AD 60–61
In Rome under guard	AD 61
Philemon, Colossians, Ephesians and Philippians written in prison	AD 61
Released and free to travel	AD 62–66
1 Timothy and Titus written	AD 62–65
Paul arrested and imprisoned in Rome	AD 66–67
2 Timothy written from prison	AD 67
Paul executed	AD 67

WHY DID HE WRITE HIS LETTERS?

I'm sure there's a line in a song that says 'growing up is hard to do'. Answers on a postcard to ... blah, blah, blah. If the line exists it's certainly true, and it's never any harder than in the teenage years.

The churches Paul had started were growing up at a fast rate. And, like human teenagers, the growing up involved pushing some boundaries and getting into some trouble.

The churches looked to Paul, the person who had 'founded' them, as a kind of father figure, and they expected his help. As he couldn't be everywhere at once, he often wrote letters.

BUT ARE THEY REALLY LETTERS?

Paul would have got top marks from his English teacher (or, to be more accurate, his Greek teacher) for letter composition. All his letters are written in the correct ancient style and form.

Paul probably dictated them to a professional secretary or scribe, who often seemed to find it hard to keep up with the rushing Paul. As this person wrote with aching hands and fingers, I bet he wished someone had invented laptops!

Because Paul feared letters might be forged in his name, he often wrote the last few lines himself to act as a signature.

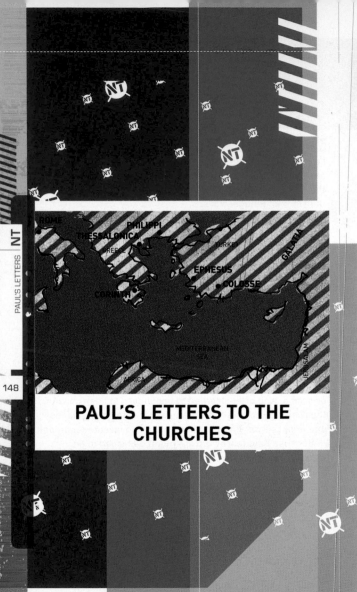

ROME
PHILIPPI
THESSALONICA
GREECE
TURKEY
GALATIA
EPHESUS
COLOSSE
CORINTH
MEDITERRANEAN SEA
AFRICA
JERUSALEM

PAUL'S LETTERS TO THE CHURCHES

THE LETTER TO THE
ROMANS

THE CITY OF ROME

Geography – Rome was the centre of the universe, or of the massive Roman Empire at least. In the ancient world it was said that all roads led to Rome.

Population – Rome was also the largest city in the world, with between one and four million people. The capital attracted men and women from every country, and wealthy kings and lords mixed on every street with beggars and slaves.

Politics – There was a new emperor, Nero, and his guards and soldiers were everywhere, carrying out his wishes not just in the city but throughout the whole world.

THE CHURCH IN ROME

One ancient historian must have failed his spelling tests – he records that the Emperor Claudius threw all the Jews out of Rome because they had been rioting about someone called 'Chrestus'. This must be a misspelt Latin form of Christ. The historian tells us that the church in Rome had begun before the end of Claudius' reign.

Like the people of many capital cities, it seems that the Roman Christians were proud. This caused friction as both Jews and Gentiles wanted to be in charge.

WHY DID PAUL WRITE THIS LETTER?

'Now, let me think ... I could invite myself around to stay with some wealthy Roman Christians for a few weeks. Then I could take up a collection and that would pay for a nice holiday on the Costa del Sol in sunny Spain. Bingo – it's a plan!'

I wouldn't dare to imply that that was how the great apostle Paul thought, but that was roughly his purpose in writing the letter to the Romans. He wanted to establish contact and prepare the Romans for his coming to stay. And one of his hopes was that the wealthy people of the capital city would be able to provide him with money to go on another, even more far-reaching, missionary journey to Spain.

THE OTHER SIDE OF THE CONVERSATION

By studying Paul's letter to the Romans, we can tell that these are the questions they had been asking him:

1. **How should Christians treat government authorities?**
2. **How can something as invisible as 'faith' save you?**
3. **If we're completely forgiven, do we still have to obey rules?**
4. **Are Jewish Christians better off with God than Gentiles?**

As you read through Romans, see if you can see where Paul is answering these questions.

MAIN THEMES

GREAT SAVE!

American cheerleaders sometimes chant this phrase at opposition teams in the hope of psyching them out: 'We are dynamite – don't mess with dynamite'. It might not win music industry awards for lyrics, but it is effective.

The book of Romans has been compared to dynamite, and at the risk of psyching you out, I'd say to you don't read it unless you're ready for your life to be changed. Great church leaders like Martin Luther, who started the Reformation, and John Wesley, were both deeply affected by the book of Romans. So what got to them?

The teaching that most affected them was that Christians are saved not by any action we take, but because of what Jesus has already done. According to Paul, we are saved by faith alone. That may not seem too radical to you, but in other stages of the Church's history it was explosive stuff.

BUT WHAT ABOUT ME?

We are saved because of Jesus, not because of anything we've done. We can't earn God's love by doing good stuff, but our actions should show that we know Him.

⭐ INTERESTING BITS ||||||||||||||||||||||||||||

Downward spiral of humanity without God
– Read Romans 1:18–32
Nothing can separate us from God's love
– Read Romans 8:28–39
Practical advice for living – Read Romans 12:1–15:17

LETTERS TO THE CHURCHES AND REGIONS

THE LETTERS TO THE CORINTHIANS

THE CITY OF CORINTH

Geography – Corinth was situated on a very narrow strip of land between the two parts of Greece. Small boats were actually dragged from one side to the other on rollers.

Population – It was a large and very busy city with around 700,000 people. There was a particularly high number of slaves in Corinth.

Politics – At the time of Paul's letters, Corinth was an important Roman colony and the capital of the Roman province of Achaia.

Sports – Corinth held a famous 'games', second only to the Olympics in popularity.

Religion – Corinth was a pagan city, although there were also Jews there. The most important deity was the goddess Aphrodite, goddess of love and beauty.

Morality – If Corinth were a film, it would be rated an '18'. One writer has said that Corinth was 'a seaman's paradise, a drunkard's heaven, and a virtuous woman's hell'.

THE CHURCH

Paul had spent one and a half years in Corinth (Acts 18), and had started the church, but it always seemed to have its problems.

There were both Jews and Greeks among the believers, but perhaps unsurprisingly in such an immoral city, the new believers seemed to struggle with Christian conduct. Sexual sins seem to have been a particular problem for the Corinthians, so there is much that we can learn from these letters to help us in our sex-crazed society.

1 CORINTHIANS

WHY DID PAUL WRITE THIS LETTER?

Have you ever had a friend who was so competitive that you couldn't put your socks on or pick your nose without it becoming a competition? 'Mine's bigger and greener than yours!' Some people are competitive to the point of insanity.

The Corinthians were like that, and they carried the competitive attitudes of their famous sporting games into church with them. Paul heard of rivalries among leaders in the church, and also received a letter asking specific questions. He was worried, and so he wrote 1 Corinthians to them.

THE OTHER SIDE OF THE CONVERSATION

From Paul's response, we can guess at some of the questions that the people of Corinth asked him. Here are some of the key ones:

1. **Is it all right to argue over who's the best Christian leader?**
2. **Is marriage a good or a bad thing?**
3. **How can we use spiritual gifts without it becoming a competition?**

Look for Paul's answers to these questions when you read 1 Corinthians.

MAIN THEME

Large companies sometimes employ professional problem solvers called 'trouble-shooters'. Don't worry – it's all legal and above board. They're not hitmen paid to 'shoot' or 'take out' troublesome workers. Their job is to use their experience to make the company work better in areas where there are major hold-ups.

The main theme of 1 Corinthians is the various troubles in the church. Practically everything Paul says in this letter is correcting the way things are done, or the way people thought in the Corinthian church. Paul is working as a trouble-shooter.

 BUT WHAT ABOUT ME?

1 Corinthians is all about how to choose a godly lifestyle when everyone around seems to be selfish, proud and just out to please themselves. Sounds useful to me.

 INTERESTING BITS ||||||||||||||||||||||||||||||

Paul's view of marriage – Read 1 Corinthians 7:1–40
The famous love chapter – Read 1 Corinthians 13:1–13
The resurrection = victory over death
– Read 1 Corinthians 15:1–58

2 CORINTHIANS

WHY DID PAUL WRITE THE SECOND LETTER?

Ever seen a Laurel and Hardy film? Although it's funny, it can be excruciatingly frustrating to watch. You know the situation is going to get worse and worse before it gets better.

Paul must have had that kind of frustrated feeling about Corinth. No matter what he did, things got worse and worse. Having written 1 Corinthians to them and made a flying visit from where he was living in Ephesus, they were still in as much of a mess as ever. It seems in the end he had to be very hard on them to straighten them out.

He wrote another letter, which unfortunately (or perhaps fortunately for the pride of the Corinthians) has been lost. In it he told them in no uncertain terms to sort their lives out. Finally they came round, and 2 Corinthians was written after all of that to assure them that he still loved and cared for them.

Some of the ground that Paul covered answered questions the Corinthians might have had, such as:

1. **How can we judge who is a true minister of God, if not by their talents and status?**
2. **How can we learn to view people as Jesus does and not just according to their social standing?**
3. **How can God use us when we're weak?**

Watch for answers to these questions as you read through 2 Corinthians.

MAIN THEME

Daydream break. You're leaning on a bright red Porsche convertible on the beach front in Monte Carlo. You're wearing sunglasses so expensive that they make anything else look like the plastic present from a Christmas cracker. Your clothes are straight out of *Vogue* or *GQ* magazine, and every one of the beautiful people wandering along the street stops to stare at you. OK, you can wake up now ...

It's image that counts, right? That's what a lot of people think. If I can just wear the right clothes and be seen with the right people, then life will be perfect.

That's what the Corinthians believed too. What people thought of them was more important than anything else. They had to look great, dress right, live in the right area of the city, and have a reputation for being talented at what they did. Paul still needed to straighten them out some more.

Strange as it may seem, one of the main themes of 2 Corinthians is boasting. The Corinthians were used to boasting about their wealth, their intelligence or their important positions.

Paul was very clear in telling them that these weren't the sort of things that Christians should be proud of. Paul said that Christians may only boast about their weaknesses – because this is what Christ is able to work through. That teaching must have gone straight to the heart of the proud Corinthians.

 BUT WHAT ABOUT ME?

Image, pride and reputation don't count for anything. What's really important is what God thinks of us, and what He's done for us.

 INTERESTING BITS ||||||||||||||||||||||||||||||||

Christians are like Christ's ambassadors
– Read 2 Corinthians 5:16–21
Read about all that Paul had suffered
– Read 2 Corinthians 11:16–33

THE LETTER TO THE
GALATIANS

GEOGRAPHY

This letter was written to four cities in the Roman province of Galatia that Paul visited on his first missionary journey.

WHY DID PAUL WRITE TO THE GALATIAN CHURCHES?

A friend of mine once belonged to a very elite group of swimmers. They decided that to join their group you not only had to be a fast enough swimmer, but you also had to agree to follow their rules. This included shaving all the hair off your head and body before big races. It was supposed to make you feel part of the group, and also to cut down on drag as you swam through the water. Yeah, right! Understandably, for some would-be members that was asking too much and they never joined the group.

In Galatia, the Jewish Christians were forcing the Gentile Christians to obey their Jewish rules. They said that following Jesus was not enough. If you wanted to be a real Christian you had to become a Jew.

One of their main demands was that the male converts be circumcised (an eye-watering and excruciatingly painful experience for an adult man). Totally understandably, a lot of would-be Christians thought this was a bit much. Paul was angry about what the Jewish Christians were saying, and he wrote to tell them so.

THE OTHER SIDE OF THE CONVERSATION

There were false teachers in the Galatian area who argued that Christianity was a part of the Jewish religion and therefore converts must become Jews. The questions that seemed to have reached Paul were:

1. Must Gentile converts be circumcised and live out the Jewish way of life?
2. If they refuse, are they 'second-class' Christians?

As you read Galatians, look for the points at which Paul answers these questions.

MAIN THEME ||||||||||||||||||||||||||||||||

So embarrassing! Have you ever been given a really expensive Christmas present by a friend who you didn't even think of buying for? You feel so bad that often, even though you've already been given the gift, you try to earn it. You start being incredibly nice to them, phoning them every night, making sure you invite them every time you go out, trying to set them up with your boyfriend ... OK, perhaps not that nice.

Paul had to explain to the Galatian Christians that there was nothing they could do to earn God's love and salvation. It was a free gift that He had given them, and no effort of theirs could make them deserve it.

He said it was OK if Jewish Christians wanted to go on following the Jewish laws, but that it didn't make them any better than people who didn't.

BUT WHAT ABOUT ME?

God just loves us! There's nothing you can do to earn His love, so just say thank You and enjoy it!

INTERESTING BITS ||||||||||||||||||||||||

Paul argues with Peter about the rules
– Read Galatians 2:11–21
We are not God's slaves but His children
– Read Galatians 4:1–7
This'll make your eyes water ... – Read Galatians 5:12

THE LETTER TO THE
EPHESIANS

THE CITY

Geography – Ephesus was located at the mouth of the
Cayster River. It was a busy sea port because it was the
western end of the great overland trade route to the East.

Politics – Although it wasn't the capital, Ephesus was
considered the first city because it was so busy and wealthy
– a bit like New York in the USA.

Religion – Ephesus was another pagan city and the home to
another goddess – the goddess Diana (called Artemis by the
Greeks). The temple built for the goddess in Ephesus was
one of the seven wonders of the ancient world. Her statue in
the temple was supposed to have fallen from heaven.

Entertainment – With the largest Roman theatre in Asia
Minor, as well as many other attractions, Ephesus was an
entertainment capital.

THE CHURCH

Paul spent a number of years in Ephesus on his second
and third missionary journeys. As usual, the people of the
city had a sort of love–hate relationship with him – the
Christians loved him, and everybody else hated him.

The people he particularly ticked off in Ephesus were
the craftsmen who made little souvenirs of the statue of
Diana for all the tourists. Their gripe was that Paul had let
the secret out of the bag and was telling everybody that the
Greek gods, like Diana, were 'no gods at all'.

Nobody wanted to buy pretty little statues any more, and
the craftsmen were feeling the pinch. When they rioted,
Paul wanted to preach to them, but somebody explained

that sometimes discretion is the better part of valour, and helped him to escape.

The church contained both Gentile and Jewish Christians, and in later centuries grew to become the largest and most important church in that region.

WHY DID PAUL WRITE THE LETTER?

Unlike Paul's other letters, there really is no 'other side to the conversation'. The letter is not written in response to any major problems or questions on the part of the Ephesian church. It has a positive feel, and was written by Paul during his imprisonment in Rome – when presumably he had plenty of time on his hands.

MAIN THEME

I'd never say it to their faces, but it is easy to assume that bodybuilders are thick – not only in the biceps but in the head – and that their brains, like their thighs, are solid muscle. This is certainly not fair, but you tend to think that if they're that focused on their bodies, spending hours every day in the gym, they must be neglecting their heads.

Paul often uses the analogy that Christ is the head and the Church is His body. In that case, the book of Ephesians is bodybuilder paradise.

In Ephesians, Paul concentrates on how the body of Christ, the Church, can be built up into Mr Universe-type proportions. For Paul, unity is like the latest bulk-builder high protein drink that the Ephesians need if they are to grow big and strong. He talks about unity in deep spiritual ways, but also very practically.

BUT WHAT ABOUT ME?

Unity is important. Really important. So let's value other people and do whatever we can to make our churches united.

★ INTERESTING BITS ||||||||||||||||||||||||

Paul's prayer for the Ephesians – Read Ephesians 3:14–21
Children and parents – Read Ephesians 6:1–4
Fight the spiritual battle – Read Ephesians 6:10–20

LETTERS TO THE CHURCHES AND REGIONS

THE LETTER TO THE
PHILIPPIANS

THE CITY

Geography – Philippi was in Macedonia and located on a fertile plain about ten miles inland from the Aegean Sea.

Politics – The city was named after the father of Alexander the Great, who was called Philip (obviously). It was a Roman colony, and was an important trading station as it was built on a busy road called the Ignatian Way.

Fame – It was famous for its gold deposits, and for its medical school where some people believe Luke the New Testament writer studied.

THE CHURCH

Every teacher has their favourite pupil. If you forget your homework it's double detention for sure, but if the 'little pet' should not bring it then the teacher is all concerned: 'Is everything OK? Is there anything I can do?'

If Paul had a favourite church, it would appear to have been the one at Philippi. He had started the church on his second missionary journey, and it was in Philippi that Paul and Silas were miraculously released from prison by an earthquake. So Paul undoubtedly had some fond memories of them.

As there was no Jewish synagogue in Philippi, it is likely that the Christians were all Gentiles.

Like all good, well mannered children, Paul had been taught to write 'thank you' notes for gifts he received. His granny got one, so did Aunty Maude, and also the Philippian church. It's apparently not the first time they supported him, although I'm sure that had nothing to do with their status as 'teacher's pet'.

Their latest gift gets this 'thank you' letter, with a few added morsels of theology.

THE OTHER SIDE OF THE CONVERSATION

Epaphroditus, who carried the gift to Paul, obviously had information on how the church was going in Philippi. He could have asked Paul any questions that the Christians had. Their concerns seem to have been:

1. **How are you doing, Paul? We (the Philippians) are worried about your suffering. (Doesn't that sound just like a teacher's pet!)**
2. **What sort of conduct does Christ's humility require of His followers?**
3. **Are you quite sure that we don't need to become Jews?**

As you read Philippians look for Paul's answers to these questions.

MAIN THEME

The school outing to the theme park has been cancelled, and an exam is scheduled in its place. What you really need is a period of feeling sorry for yourself, a day of black moods so that everyone knows how unlucky you are. But there's always some cheery, ever-pleasant person who wants to tell you to count your blessings and look on the bright side – after all, every cloud has a silver lining. But all you want to do is strangle them.

The main theme of Philippians is joy. Although Paul is in prison and could soon be executed, he is still joyful and unconcerned – to live is Christ, to die is gain (1:21). He wants the Philippians to experience the same joy that he has.

BUT WHAT ABOUT ME?

Compared to knowing Jesus, everything else is rubbish! So even if life gets really hard, we can still have real joy if we know Him.

Jesus gave us an incredible example of how to be humble. Let's follow it.

INTERESTING BITS ||||||||||||||||||||||||||||||

A hymn of the Early Church about Jesus
– Read Philippians 2:5–11
Paul's early successes are rubbish compared to knowing Jesus – Read Philippians 3:4–11

LETTERS TO THE CHURCHES AND REGIONS

THE LETTER TO THE COLOSSIANS

THE CITY

Geography – The city lies in the valley of the Lycus River in a mountainous region about 100 miles east of Ephesus.

History – Colosse may have started its life as a military fort because it was strategically placed in a defendable valley on an important trade route.

Fame – 'Hey, look at those weird purple sheep!' Colosse was famous for its sheep, whose wool had a purple tinge and could be sold for lots and lots of money.

THE CHURCH

'If Dad's out of his depth, perhaps Granddad can help' seems to be the thought of the Colossians.

Paul had not started or even visited the church in Colosse. It seems that it had been founded by a man named Epaphras who had been converted by Paul in Ephesus, and who had then gone back to his home town of Colosse.

The problems in Colosse were obviously too big for him to handle, so he travelled all the way to Rome to ask the advice of Paul, his father in the faith and a sort of granddaddy to the church.

WHY DID PAUL WRITE TO THE COLOSSIANS?

It seemed that a particular false teaching had entered the church in Colosse. The weird ideas of what might have been a sort of Christian secret society included:
• believing that secret information saves you
• not thinking that Christ was very important
• worshipping angels as messengers between man and God
• following some of the Jewish laws and customs.

THE OTHER SIDE OF THE CONVERSATION

For Epaphras to travel all the way to Rome from Colosse shows that he was pretty desperate – there were no non-stop flights in those days! When he got to Paul he would undoubtedly have made the most of the opportunity to pick his brains.

From the letter that Paul sent back to Colosse it seems that these were the questions he was asking:

1. How can I tell which religious leader to listen to?
2. How should a real Christian live?
3. Is there secret knowledge that only some Christians know?

As you read, see how Paul responded to these questions.

 MAIN THEME ||||||||||||||||||||||||||||||

If the French Revolution taught us nothing else, it taught us (thanks to the invention of the guillotine) that bodies no longer connected to their heads die. (Some reports say it took a few seconds – eyes in unattached heads looking around, and even mouths speaking.)

If Ephesians was the bodybuilders' letter, then Colossians is the letter about the importance of the head. Paul focuses his attention on Christ as the Head of the Church, because the Colossians had begun to doubt His importance.

Paul stresses that Christ is always the most important, because He maintains the whole universe and saves humanity, as well as overseeing the Church.

BUT WHAT ABOUT ME?

Jesus first always. If anyone says otherwise, don't listen to them!

INTERESTING BITS ||||||||||||||||||||||||||||||

Christ, Master of the universe – Read Colossians 1:15–20
How Christians should live – Read Colossians 3:1–17

LETTERS TO THE CHURCHES AND REGIONS

THE LETTERS TO THE
THESSALONIANS

THE CITY

Geography – Thessalonica is a natural harbour and in Paul's time was the capital city of the Roman province of Macedonia.

Population – Thessalonica was an important trading city, and there were many non-native inhabitants, including Jews.

THE CHURCH

Paul spent about one month in Thessalonica on his second missionary journey. He was forced to leave because the unbelieving Jews were rioting and trying to kill him. He left some of his helpers behind to continue the work, and a church made up mostly of Gentiles was started.

1 THESSALONIANS

WHY DID PAUL WRITE THE FIRST LETTER TO THE THESSALONIANS?

Have you ever seen news reports about the street children of South America? Five- and six-year-olds living alone on the streets, stealing and fighting to stay alive. Harsh conditions force children to grow up fast.

Paul wrote this first letter only a few weeks after he had left the Thessalonians, so they were baby Christians, but in an environment of violent persecution they were having to grow up fast. Paul wrote to encourage them in their new faith, and to tell them about the great Christian hope of Jesus' second coming and heaven.

THE OTHER SIDE OF THE CONVERSATION

Quite understandably, the Thessalonian Christians thought they might have made a big mistake. What kind of religion is it that can get you killed so easily? They wanted to know:

1. **What happens to Christians who die?**
2. **Is all this trouble because God is angry?**
3. **Does all this persecution have any benefits?**

See how Paul answers these questions as you read 1 Thessalonians.

MAIN THEME ||||||||||||||||||||||||||

The dentist will sometimes promise a little child a balloon as soon as he's finished poking around in their mouth. That hope might give them the strength to endure the discomfort of having ten fingers and about five tools stuck in their mouth.

In the same way, hope is the main theme of Paul's first letter to the Thessalonians. He knows they are having a hard time, and he wants to encourage them. Particularly, he encourages them by telling them that one day Jesus will come back and all Christians will go to heaven to be with Him.

BUT WHAT ABOUT ME?

Are people giving you a hard time for being a Christian? Paul's advice to the Thessalonians could help you.

INTERESTING BITS ||||||||||||||||||||

They are an example of good converts
– Read 1 Thessalonians 1:4–10
Be encouraged: Jesus will return
– Read 1 Thessalonians 4:13–5:11

2 THESSALONIANS

WHY DID PAUL WRITE THE SECOND LETTER TO THE THESSALONIANS?

Have you ever been under so much pressure that you actually thought you were going to lose it? You start to have visions of accidentally introducing yourself as Napoleon, or forgetting to dress before you leave for school in the morning.

Well, the young Thessalonian Christians were under so much pressure that they became fanatics. They wanted Jesus to come back and save them from persecution so much that they made themselves believe that they could practically hear Him coming.

If the Thessalonians were to calm down, they needed answers to questions like these:

1. **Why doesn't God punish evil people who hurt Christians?**
2. **Is it true that we're in the final evil days of the anti-Christ?**

Every so often, whenever the times seem particularly turbulent or strange, some Christians become fanatical about predicting Jesus' return. As you read 2 Thessalonians, see what Paul has to say about that.

MAIN THEME

Have you ever asked yourself: 'Is it worth it?' Perhaps as you sat down to another evening's intensive revision, or as you pumped out your 200th press-up. 'Can passing my exams or getting onto the team possibly be worth this?' In 2 Thessalonians Paul says, 'Don't give up – stand firm!' Like an athletics coach, he encouraged them to keep going to the end!

BUT WHAT ABOUT ME?

Even when following Jesus gets really hard, keep going! It really *is* worth it!

INTERESTING BITS

Encouragement to keep going
– Read 2 Thessalonians 2:13–17
Christians should not be lazy
– Read 2 Thessalonians 3:6–15

THE LETTERS TO
TIMOTHY

WHO WAS TIMOTHY?

Little brothers and sisters can have you tearing your hair out as they tag along and copy you. But it's also quite nice to know that however much they might try to hide it, there's a bit of hero worship going on – with you as the hero!

Timothy was something of a little brother to Paul, or a son in the faith as Paul puts it. He became a Christian under Paul's ministry and then insisted on tagging along with him on his second and third missionary journeys. Soon Paul trusted Timothy enough to appoint him the leader of the growing church in Ephesus.

1 TIMOTHY

WHY DID PAUL WRITE 1 TIMOTHY?

There are two ways of making a model. You can simply spread the parts all over the floor, pick up the biggest and most interesting bits, and start gluing. (That was always my method, which possibly explains why everything I made came out looking the same – a mixture between a double-decker bus and a deformed elephant.) Or you can read the instructions and proceed in a step by step manner.

As a young man with a very big job on his hands, Timothy needed all the help he could get. His big brother didn't let him down. Paul wrote 1 Timothy to him, giving him some step-by-step advice on how to get the church up and running.

MAIN THEME |||||||||||||||||||||||||||||||||||

Just wanting something isn't enough, or I'd have played rugby for England long ago. You have to have the necessary qualities.

Paul's instructions to Timothy showed him what it was that made a good Christian leader. It is not wrong, said Paul, to want to be a leader, but as well as the desire you must have other qualifications. Leaders must be respected inside and outside the church, they mustn't be too new a Christian, and they must be self-controlled.

BUT WHAT ABOUT ME?

We might not all be leaders, but we can all set an example to other Christians. Read 1 Timothy to find out how.

INTERESTING BITS ||||||||||||||||||||||||||||||

Qualifications for Christian leaders
– Read 1 Timothy 3:1–13
Being satisfied is being truly wealthy
– Read 1 Timothy 6:3–10
The challenge to all Christian youth
– Read 1 Timothy 6:11–21

2 TIMOTHY

WHY DID PAUL WRITE 2 TIMOTHY?

I can remember a moment of stunned silence in an international athletics meeting. It was the men's 4 x 100m relay, and the English team were doing so well. The third runner took off, and it looked as if we were in with a real chance. Then the stunned silence ... the crowd realised that the baton wasn't in the runner's hand. It had been dropped and the race was over.

2 Timothy was the last letter Paul wrote, and when he wrote it he knew that his death was near. As an old leader, he knew the baton must be handed over to someone younger and it must not be dropped. So he wrote to encourage Timothy to keep going no matter how hard things were, and to continue the work that Paul had started.

MAIN THEME ||||||||||||||||||||||||||||||||

If you've ever played with a terrier dog, you'll know why they have a reputation for never giving up. Once it's got that toy in its mouth you're never going to get it back again. Paul wrote to Timothy to encourage him to be persistent. He used the example of soldiers, farmers and athletes to persuade Timothy to keep going no matter what the cost.

BUT WHAT ABOUT ME?

We should always be prepared to tell people about Jesus. It's even more important when they're surrounded by trendy but wrong ideas. Living for Jesus and telling people about Him might not make us popular, but we must keep going, whatever happens.

INTERESTING BITS |||||||||||||||||||||||||||||

Paul remembers Timothy's background
– Read 2 Timothy 1:3–7
Timothy, the soldier of Christ Jesus – Read 2 Timothy 2:1–7

THE LETTER TO
TITUS

BACKGROUND

Have you ever had the feeling that all the worst jobs have some kind of homing device directing them straight at you? It's classroom clean-up time at the end of term. Fred's taking text books back to the store room. Others are auctioning off the contents of the lost property cupboard to the highest bidder. And you? You're pulling used, and still sticky, bits of chewing gum off the underside of desks – with your teeth!

Titus must have had a similar feeling. His friend Timothy is in Ephesus – beautiful city, wonderful people, pleasure capital of the world. And him? He's assigned to a little rock in the middle of the sea called Crete.

What's Crete famous for? It's famous for inhabitants that are lazy, compulsive liars, and talented at nothing but eating. Just the place to be assigned to as a church leader. Paul must have known that he'd given Titus the short end of the stick because he quickly wrote to him with some tips on how to get by.

MAIN THEMES

Do you know any hypocrites? (Be careful as you answer that question – you never know if someone else's finger might be pointing back at you.) Probably we all know a hypocrite or two.

Lots of people have said that they think Jesus was great, and that they'd willingly be His followers if it weren't for the fact that all the Christians they know are hypocrites. This is something we as Christians need to consider carefully.

Paul knew the way the Cretans lived, and he told Titus to make sure that any who became Christians changed their lifestyle as well as their beliefs. He didn't want Titus to have any hypocrites in his church.

BUT WHAT ABOUT ME?

Do your actions measure up to your words? It's important that they do …

⭐ **INTERESTING BITS** |||||||||||||||||||||||||||||

Advice for different groups of people – Read Titus 2:1–10
Christians should live good lives – Read Titus 3:1–10

LETTERS TO INDIVIDUALS

THE LETTER TO
PHILEMON

BACKGROUND

There's an old joke that goes: What's worse than biting into an apple and finding a worm? Answer: Biting into an apple and finding half a worm!

Things are not always as good as they appear on the surface. The Roman Empire looked like a civilised society on the surface, but beneath the 'skin' of happy, wealthy people was a core of brutality and many, many poor and powerless men and women. Some of the most cruelly treated were the slaves.

The very short letter to Philemon concerns a slave called Onesimus who had run away from his master. This meant that if he was ever caught he could immediately be executed.

Hiding out in Rome, the biggest and busiest city, where questions were least likely to be asked, Onesimus ran into Paul and was converted. Through coincidence, or perhaps 'God-incidence', Paul knew the slave's master, a man called Philemon. Philemon was also a believer, so Paul wrote to him.

MAIN THEME ||||||||||||||||||||||||||||||||

The main theme of Philemon is the relationship between Christians. By law Philemon, as Onesimus's master, had the right to kill him for what he had done. But Paul argues that you can't do that because he's now your brother in Christ. Paul demonstrates true Christian love by offering to pay anything that Onesimus owes Philemon.

Paul asks Philemon to take Onesimus back and not to punish him. He even implies that he might like to set him free. This would be very radical behaviour for a Roman slave owner, but for Onesimus's sake we can only hope Philemon took Paul's advice.

BUT WHAT ABOUT ME?

As Christians, we are brothers and sisters. We're family. That should make a difference to how we treat each other.

INTERESTING BITS ||||||||||||||||||||||

To see how Christians should treat one another
– Read Philemon vv. 8–20

OTHER LETTERS

THE LETTER TO THE HEBREWS

INTRODUCTION

When artists paint, they choose one central point as their focus. Everything else in the picture guides the viewer's eye towards that point.

In Hebrews, Jesus is seen as the focus towards which all of the history of the world points.

WHO WROTE HEBREWS?

Trying to decide who wrote Hebrews is like trying to pick the one criminal from a line-up of likely suspects, including: Paul, Barnabas, Luke, Apollos, Silas, or even Priscilla – who as a woman might have chosen not to put her name to the letter because of the prejudice against her sex (but wouldn't she have called it 'Shebrews'?).

We will never know for certain who wrote Hebrews until they 'fess up in heaven.

WHO WAS IT WRITTEN TO?

Like Paul's letters, the title 'Hebrews' reflects the people it was thought to have been written to – that is, Jewish/Hebrew Christians. It was most likely written to the Hebrew Christians in Rome some time in the sixties of the first century AD.

WHY WAS IT WRITTEN?

Have you ever noticed that it takes a conscious effort to tidy a bedroom, but no effort at all to make one messy – it just happens. Next time your mother complains, you can explain to her that it is due to the 'fourth law of thermodynamics' which states that if left without outside influence, systems (bedrooms) always degenerate (get messy). Check with your physics teacher – it's a real physical law.

Churches, like bedrooms, tend to go downhill. It seems that the church in Rome had been persecuted from the outside, and on the inside things were becoming messy. They had split into rival groups that didn't meet together any more.

Hebrews might have been written to a group of Jewish Christians who had gone their own way, and because of persecution were now wondering: 'Wouldn't it be better if we just went back to being normal Jews?'

'Absolutely no way, José,' is what the writer to the Hebrews told them!

MAIN THEMES

'This is no upgrade – we're talking a whole new model here.'

Most computers today can be upgraded. Simply take out the old component and put in a new one. If you upgraded your computer with the latest state of the art, super-dooper processor, but then found it was more trouble than it was worth – you'd take it back, demand a refund, and get your good, old chip back, wouldn't you?

It seems that this was how the Hebrews felt. They'd tried this newfangled Christianity, and frankly they were pretty unimpressed. They hadn't planned on having to be polite to those Gentile types for one thing, and persecution was definitely not what they had signed up for.

The writer to the Hebrews had to straighten them out. Jesus wasn't just an alternative to the old way of doing things. He was superior in every way and to every person that the Jews respected in the Old Testament.

This wasn't just an upgrade – it was a whole new way of doing things. Now that God had put the new system on the market, He wasn't supporting the old one. It was: do it the new and better way, or don't do it at all.

JESUS AS PRIEST AND SACRIFICE

'Oh, that is such a sweet little lamb. What are you going to do with it? No, you're joking! You're not going to ... Did I hear someone mention mint sauce?'

In the Old Testament, priests offered animal sacrifices to cover people's sins – but of course this didn't really do away with sin; it was simply a sign of what would one day happen. The real sacrifice for sin was when Jesus died on the cross. The book of Hebrews explains how this worked.

BUT WHAT ABOUT ME?

When we choose to follow Jesus, He turns our world upside down. He's bigger and better than anything else, ever! So knowing Him should make a difference to our whole lives.

INTERESTING BITS

Jesus, the better 'great high priest'
– Read Hebrews 4:14–16
A better agreement between God and man
– Read Hebrews 8:1–13
Great men and women of faith – Read Hebrews 11:1–40
Christians should follow Jesus' example
– Read Hebrews 12:1–13:17

THE LETTER OF
JAMES

INTRODUCTION

'Just do it!' It might be a slogan for trainers now, but James could well win the court battle for the right to it, as he coined the expression 2,000 years ago. His advice was: if you want to be a real Christian, don't talk about it ... just do it!

WHO WROTE IT?

'Sibling rivalry' is what polite sociologists call it. 'World War Three' might be more appropriate for what goes on in some families. Brothers and sisters might love one another, but that doesn't stop them fighting. If you've got a juicy zit on your forehead, then no one's going to enjoy telling you more than your big brother. If a girl phoned to say that actually she's changed her mind and she'd rather contract bubonic plague than go to the cinema with you, then you can bet your little sister is going to enjoy giving you the message.

One of the most amazing evidences for the truth of Jesus' claims is that His family came to believe that He really was God. He must have been quite an incredible brother!

There is more than one James mentioned in the New Testament, but only one is a standout contender for author of this book – that is, James the half brother of Jesus. He was the son of Mary and Joseph, but only half brother to Jesus because Jesus was conceived in the womb of Mary by the power of the Holy Spirit.

After Jesus' death and resurrection, James joined the Church and became one of the Jerusalem leaders.

WHAT BECAME OF JAMES?

The historian Eusebius tells us that James prayed so much he had knees as tough as a camel's. In an attempt to make him give up his faith, the Jewish leaders dragged him to the top of the Temple in Jerusalem. When he got there, instead of admitting that he was wrong, he started to preach about Jesus. They responded by throwing him off. When that didn't kill him, they stoned him.

Since he was martyred in AD 62, we know the book of James must have been written before then.

WHO WAS IT WRITTEN TO?

The first verse of James states that the book is written to Jewish believers who 'are scattered among the nations'. They had probably been scattered because of the persecution in Jerusalem.

James obviously felt that they needed some encouragement, not only to make it through the persecution, but to live lives that reflected their Christian faith.

⊙ MAIN THEME ||||||||||||||||||||||||||||||

Doctors and nurses have some rather unpleasant methods of deciding how deeply unconscious a patient is. They might stick pins into them, or, if they're feeling compassionate, they might just give their earlobe a good hard pinch.

James had his own test to see if someone's faith was really alive. He said that what we believe will come out in how we act. To paraphrase: if you don't act like a Christian, you're not a Christian. Ouch!

The areas that he was particularly interested in included: resisting temptation; treating everyone equally, whether they are rich or poor; controlling what we say; and having the right attitude to money. All of these issues are very much alive and kicking today.

👤 BUT WHAT ABOUT ME?

Do you believe in Jesus? Yes? Great! But do your actions show that?

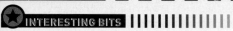

Don't just listen, act – Read James 1:19–27
Treat everyone equally, whether rich or poor
– Read James 2:1–13
The power of words – Read James 3:1–12
The power of prayer – Read James 5:13–18

THE LETTERS OF
PETER

WHO WROTE THEM?

If the central characters of the New Testament were to be given Olympic medals, the author of these letters, Peter, might well get silver (Jesus gets gold, of course). He was one of Jesus' first disciples, and the leader on which Jesus said He would build His Church.

These letters were probably written from Rome (which Peter refers to in the letters as Babylon – perhaps it was a code to keep his whereabouts secret) sometime around AD 65.

WHAT HAPPENED TO PETER?

Tradition says that Peter was martyred in Rome. The Romans intended to crucify Peter, but he was so humble that he didn't believe he was worthy to die in the same way as his Lord Jesus. So, at his request they crucified him upside down.

WHO DID HE WRITE HIS LETTERS TO?

When they try, the Post Office are actually very good at deciphering bad or incomplete addresses on letters, but they would have had trouble with Peter's letters. They simply say – To: Christians. Where: spread all over the place. Fortunately, he would have sent them with a special messenger and not Postman Pat.

1 PETER

WHY DID HE WRITE IT?

What would you be willing to give up for the man or woman you love? Talk is easy: 'I'd give up everything for you; I'd even die for you.' In real life it's more like: 'I might miss a repeat of *Friends* for you. Just this once, though, and only if you promise to let me borrow the DVD at the weekend.'

It wasn't talk for the Early Christians, though. Right from the beginning they knew that if they got involved with this Jesus character, they would have to be willing to give up everything – often even their lives. Peter wrote to help people struggling with the cost of following Jesus.

MAIN THEME

BEING THE SECOND IS ALWAYS EASIER

Potholing – I hate it. If God had intended for me to crawl through freezing, wet, narrow holes in the ground he could have made me a worm. Fortunately, on my one potholing experience I had a much bigger friend in front of me. I kept telling myself, if he could fit through that tiny, little gap and not become stuck, then it must be possible for me.

Peter reminded the persecuted Christians that they were following their Lord Jesus who had also suffered. His death on the cross was the ultimate example of unjust suffering, but it made it possible for all humanity to be brought back into relationship with God. So, Peter reminds his readers that Jesus understands and He's there with you.

BUT WHAT ABOUT ME?

1 Peter gives us real encouragement and some great advice on how to keep standing up for God in the face of persecution.

We are God's chosen people – Read 1 Peter 2:4–10
The beauty of a holy woman – Read 1 Peter 3:1–6
Special advice for young men – Read 1 Peter 5:5–11

2 PETER

WHY DID HE WRITE IT?

If you've ever had an enemy you'll know that there are two ways they can attack you: the obvious 'bash your face in' way, and the subtle 'spread vicious lies through the whole school' way.

The Early Church, like the Church today, had a very real enemy – Satan. In his first letter, Peter dealt with the enemy's obvious method – persecution. In 2 Peter, he deals with the enemy's sly, subtle attack on the Church – false teaching.

🔘 MAIN THEME ||||||||||||||||||||||||||||||||

By the age of sixteen you really ought to be able to make your own decisions about what clothes you wear. 'But, Mum, I don't really like wearing grey socks and brown sandals any more. What's more, my girlfriend hates them!' Part of growing up is learning to make your own choices.

Peter lays the facts in front of the Christians as plainly as he can, and then allows them to make their choices. They must decide between what he and those who actually saw and knew Jesus are teaching, and what the new false teachers are saying.

👤 BUT WHAT ABOUT ME?

Be careful who you listen to. Does what they say agree with what the Bible teaches us? Is their lifestyle what it should be?

THE LETTERS OF
JOHN

WHO WAS JOHN?

The writer of these letters is almost certainly the same as the writer of John's Gospel – the disciple whom Jesus loved. These might be the last of the New Testament writings, and as tradition tells us that John finished his life in the city of Ephesus, they were probably written from that city around the end of the first century AD.

John seems to have been a very gentle and loving man. In his letters he constantly refers to the people he is writing to as his 'little children'. This friendly form of speaking means that he probably knew most of them, and so these letters were most likely written to members of the churches dotted around Ephesus.

WHY DID HE WRITE THE LETTERS?

With the ever-improving abilities of everyday computers and printers, the counterfeiting of money is becoming an increasing problem. Recently in America there was a case of high school and college students working together to counterfeit hundreds of thousands of dollars. Don't even think about trying it, and especially don't ever say I gave you the idea!

Apparently, the special agents who are trained to find

counterfeit money are not given weeks of lectures on the great counterfeiters of the past, or shown all the best counterfeit notes ever produced. Instead, they spend all their time working with, looking at, feeling and touching real notes. In the end, they know them so well that they almost have a sixth sense of what is real and what is counterfeit.

John, like Peter, wrote his letters to counter false teaching. Instead of spending a lot of time talking about what the false teachers were saying, he chose to write down the truth for his readers. He hoped that they would come to know the truth so well that when false, or counterfeit, teaching came along they would instantly recognise it for what it was.

1 JOHN

It seems that when men and women grow old they have two options: they can either become soft and sentimental, or they can become really hard and bitter. I hope for your sake that your grandparents are of the former type. John certainly was.

For John, the key word is always love. He talks of the love that God has for all of us, His children, and also of the love that Christians should have for one another.

He then gives three ways that you can know a true Christian as opposed to a counterfeit one. True Christians will love other Christians, they will live righteously, and they will agree that Jesus was really man and God.

 BUT WHAT ABOUT ME?

God loves us. We should love other people. Simple really.

INTERESTING BITS |||||||||||||||||||||||||||||

We are God's children – Read 1 John 3:1–10
Love comes from God – Read 1 John 4:7–21

2 AND 3 JOHN

These two letters are both very short and very personal.

2 John is addressed to a 'chosen lady and her children'. This is probably not a real single-parent family, but is another way of referring to a church (the chosen lady) and the members (her children). John encourages the church to go on growing in love, but not to be naive. They are not to welcome into their homes people who do not teach the truth.

3 John is written to a particular church leader. When you read it, you can almost imagine that it is a modern letter. John commends his friend on all the good he is doing, but warns him against a particular church leader who is up to no good.

BUT WHAT ABOUT ME?

Walk in truth. Stay close to Jesus, and don't listen to anyone who tries to lure you away from Him.

Imitate what is good. If you see someone who's doing good, copy them!

INTERESTING BITS

There are only 27 verses altogether. Just read them, for goodness' sake!

THE LETTER OF
JUDE

WHO WAS JUDE?

Some people are such name droppers. They manage to bring their famous acquaintances into any conversation. 'Thanks for the cup of tea. Oh, that reminds me, did I tell you that I once had tea with the queen?'

Jude was not a name dropper, though he could have dropped a bigger name than most. He calls himself a brother of James, and a servant of Jesus Christ. The James he mentions is likely to be the leader of the church in Jerusalem, the writer of the book of James, and the half brother of Jesus.

As Jesus had another brother called Jude, it makes sense that this was him. He was just being modest by not mentioning the fact that he was Jesus' brother as well as His servant!

WHY DID HE WRITE IT?

Well-organised people have their business categorised into jobs that have to be done today, this week, this month, and so on. I seem to work more along the lines of things I should have done yesterday, things I should have done last week, things I should have done last month, and back through time.

It seems that Jude had been intending to write a proper, longer book, but the situation had become so bad that he had to get this one off the end of his quill and into the post as quickly as possible.

MAIN THEME

Once again the subject is false teachers. Rather than talking a lot about what they were actually teaching, he chooses to focus on the fate that awaits them – the terrible judgment of God. Thinking about that should be enough to keep sensible Christians well clear of them.

BUT WHAT ABOUT ME?

Again, think about who's influencing you, and whether they're worth listening to.

INTERESTING BITS

A wonderful prayer of hope for all of us
– Read Jude vv. 24–25

REVELATION

INTRODUCTION

Like all the best shows, the Bible goes out with bang. No book is as exciting, as dramatic or as confusing as the final one.

WHO WROTE IT?

The book of Revelation was written by the apostle John, who also wrote John's Gospel and the three letters of John.

WHEN AND WHERE DID HE WRITE IT?

Nobody likes their prisoners to escape – it just completely defeats the object. One popular trick has been to send the prisoners you're really worried about to a small island like Alcatraz or Patmos. Patmos?

Patmos was where the Romans sent political prisoners. John was there because of his Christian faith, but he managed to escape. Not literally – through a tunnel, or by taking a long swim – but through a series of visions that took him from the rocky little island up into heaven. There he was fortunate enough to be given a guided tour by Jesus Himself.

The book of Revelation is the record of these visions or revelations – revelations, get it? It was most probably written around the middle of the last decade of the first century AD.

WHO WAS IT WRITTEN FOR?

The second and third chapters of Revelation give prophecies to seven churches in the Roman province of Asia. They were probably the first, but not the last, people to receive the written form of John's visions.

WHY WAS IT WRITTEN?

If you were to tell a friend that you 'worshipped' the president, they would assume that you admired his politics. If you tried again and explained that actually you 'worshipped' him as your god, they would think that your lift didn't reach the top floor.

In Roman times the belief that the emperor was god was widespread. When Revelation was written the emperor actually required that everyone worship him. This got the Christians into a lot of hot water, because they refused to worship anyone other than Jesus.

John wrote his visions down as a book because he believed that persecuted Christians would find them comforting and that they would bring hope.

MAIN THEMES ||||||||||||||||||||||||||||||||||

UNDERSTANDING REVELATION

If your family has ever bought a new TV or computer, you'll know that everyone has their own theory as to what the instruction manual means. Even your two-year-old sister has her idea – you have to lick it, wipe your nose on it and tear it into little pieces before you can really understand it.

Revelation is about as simple to understand as a Japanese electronics instruction manual – that is, not very! There are many very different ideas as to how it is best understood. Does it describe events already past, or still to come? Or is it just poetic language that doesn't relate to the real world at all?

If you're interested, you'll have to find your own answers to those questions.

CARTOONS AND CARICATURES

Name your favourite comic book. Is it *Superman*? *Spiderman*? Or the old favourite, the *Beano*? Cartoons are a special kind of writing that we understand. We know how to make sense of them – how to uncover the joke.

The book of Revelation is also a special type of writing, one that the people to whom John was writing would have understood. It was called Apocalyptic writing. Like our modern cartoons, it often used impossible or strange creations, or caricatures of real people, rather than straightforward descriptions. In part, this was a sort of code, and in part, it just made the book more dramatic.

Although Revelation can be hard for us to understand, there are some themes on which everyone will agree.

TO THE CHURCHES

Few situations are as potentially embarrassing as those when you're sure you're alone, but actually you're not. Maybe you've got three fingers and both thumbs up one nostril, chasing the big one, and the boy you fancy walks around the corner. Or you're practising your most macho smile in the mirror, and as your focus shifts you suddenly realise all the office workers on the other side of the glass are staring at you.

The seven churches of Asia probably had no idea how close a watch was being kept on them from above. When John sent them this little 'report card' from Jesus, with their successes, failures and areas for improvement all written down, I bet they decided to smarten up their acts.

I KNOW WHAT HAPPENS!

Some films can be watched again and again. But not detective stories. If you know who did it, and why and how, there's not much excitement in following Miss Marple around her small English village.

However, in real life there are times when knowing how it's all going to turn out would be very welcome and would save us a lot of worry and sweat. 'Will she say yes, or won't she?' 'Have I passed or failed?' 'Will the latest X-Factor winner make the Christmas No. 1?' And so on.

God gave John the revelations He did because the persecuted Christians of the Early Church needed to know that however bad things seemed, it was going to be all right in the end. So, in the midst of all the weird and wonderful creatures, pictures and stories of the book of Revelation is a very simple message: God's in control, and we win!

BUT WHAT ABOUT ME?

Revelation gives us an awesome picture of what the end will be like. Whatever happens in the meantime, God's in control and He's going to make everything brilliant in the end!

★ INTERESTING BITS |||||||||||||||||||||||||||

Description of Jesus in heaven
– Read Revelation 1:12–18

The messages to the seven churches
– Read Revelation 2:1–3:22

The great crowd worships at God's throne
– Read Revelation 7:9–17

The white rider, Jesus, leads His army
– Read Revelation 19:11–21

Description of the new heaven and earth
– Read Revelation 21:1–22:21

DON'T LOOK AT ME, LOOK AT HIM!

Sounds like someone who's been caught doing something suspicious, doesn't it? He's standing there uncomfortably, looking extremely guilty, and he's desperately trying to shift the blame by pointing to someone else.

Well, for one thing it's rude to point – but that's exactly what we're trying to do with this book. Let's explain.

Every author dreams of having a bestseller. Imagine, being up there in the top 10 with the new blockbuster novel, the revealing memoirs of an ageing politician and a book of exotic recipes from the latest TV chef. Interviews on telly, invitations to top literary lunches and Hollywood knocking on the door, begging to turn this masterpiece into a big-budget, blockbuster movie.

Sounds great, and maybe one day it'll happen. But not with *this* book! You see, we'd be more than happy if you forget this book once you've read it.

'What did you say?'

Yes, that's right. The only reason this book has been written is to point you to another book, a much, much better book – THE book.

Once you've put this book down, you might say: 'Hmm, that was good. I learnt a lot, laughed at some of the stories. Yes, I enjoyed that. Now I can start on that mystery novel.' But that would be the *wrong* thing to say!

Yes, of course, read that mystery novel. But if this book hasn't made you want to go to the Bible as well, then we've failed miserably and we might as well have spent our days watching reruns of soaps.

Come on, dig into the Bible. It's exciting, challenging, life-changing. And you'll hopefully find that the Bible is a book that points as well. Only this time, it points to a Person – a powerful and loving Person, who has a plan for the human race and wants us to be a part of it.

Now, I wonder who *that* Person could be? Any ideas? Hey, don't look at me. Look at Him!

National Distributors

UK: (and countries not listed below)
CWR, Waverley Abbey House, Waverley Lane, Farnham,
Surrey GU9 8EP. Tel: (01252) 784700 Outside UK (44) 1252 784700

AUSTRALIA: KI Entertainment, Unit 21 317-321 Woodpark Road,
Smithfield, New South Wales 2164. Tel: 1 800 850 777
Fax: 02 9604 3699

CANADA: David C Cook Distribution Canada, PO Box 98, 55
Woodslee Avenue, Paris, Ontario N3L 3E5. Tel: 1800 263 2664

GHANA: Challenge Enterprises of Ghana, PO Box 5723, Accra.
Tel: (021) 222437/223249 Fax: (021) 226227

HONG KONG: Cross Communications Ltd, 1/F, 562A Nathan Road,
Kowloon. Tel: 2780 1188 Fax: 2770 6229

INDIA: Crystal Communications, 10-3-18/4/1, East Marredpalli,
Secunderabad – 500026, Andhra Pradesh Tel/Fax: (040) 27737145

KENYA: Keswick Books and Gifts Ltd, PO Box 10242-00400, Nairobi.
Tel: (254) 20 312639/3870125

MALAYSIA: Canaanland, No. 25 Jalan PJU 1A/41B, NZX Commercial
Centre, Ara Jaya, 47301 Petaling Jaya, Selangor.
Tel: (03) 7885 0540/1/2 Fax: (03) 7885 0545

Salvation Book Centre (M) Sdn Bhd, 23 Jalan SS 2/64, 47300
Petaling Jaya, Selangor. Tel: (03) 78766411/78766797
Fax: (03) 78757066/78756360

NEW ZEALAND: KI Entertainment, Unit 21 317-321 Woodpark Road,
Smithfield, New South Wales 2164. Tel: 0 800 850 777
Fax: +612 9604 3699

NIGERIA: FBFM, Helen Baugh House, 96 St Finbarr's College Road,
Akoka, Lagos. Tel: (01) 7747429/4700218/825775/827264

PHILIPPINES: OMF Literature Inc, 776 Boni Avenue, Mandaluyong
City. Tel: (02) 531 2183 Fax: (02) 531 1960

SINGAPORE: Alby Commercial Enterprises Pte Ltd,
95 Kallang Avenue #04-00, AIS Industrial Building, 339420.
Tel: (65) 629 27238 Fax: (65) 629 27235

SOUTH AFRICA: Struik Christian Books, 80 MacKenzie Street,
PO Box 1144, Cape Town 8000.Tel: (021) 462 4360 Fax: (021) 461 3612

SRI LANKA: Christombu Publications (Pvt) Ltd, Bartleet House,
65 Braybrooke Place, Colombo 2. Tel: (9411) 2421073/2447665

USA: David C Cook Distribution Canada, PO Box 98,
55 Woodslee Avenue, Paris, Ontario N3L 3E5, Canada.
Tel: 1800 263 2664

For email addresses, visit the CWR website:
www.cwr.org.uk/distributors
CWR is a Registered Charity – Number 294387
CWR is a Limited Company registered in England
– Registration Number 1990308

HOW CAN THE BIBLE BE RELEVANT TO ME?

Our daily devotional will get you digging deep into God's Word and make it real. There's nothing boring about it and you get four months' worth of:

- Sections tackling Bible themes and topical issues
- Insights into the challenges you and your mates face
- Prayers, challenges and action points to help you put it all into practice

For prices and information log on to **www.cwr.org.uk/mettle**

Also available for purchase from your local Christian bookshop.

Mettle termly resources for use in youth groups are available from Youth for Christ – contact details below.

For more information about the main *Mettle* resource, produced by Youth for Christ, please contact:
Youth for Christ, Coombswood Way, Halesowen, West Midlands B62 8BH.
TEL: 0121 502 9620.
EMAIL: mettle@yfc.co.uk
WEB: www.yfcchurchresources.co.uk
British Youth for Christ is a registered charity – 263446. A company limited by guarantee. Registered in England and Wales – Registration Number 00988200.
www.yfc.co.uk